Let's Put On A Show!

A beginner's theatre handbook for young actors

ADREA GIBBS

MERIWETHER PUBLISHING LTD.
Colorado Springs, Colorado

Meriwether Publishing Ltd., Publisher
PO Box 7710
Colorado Springs, CO 80933-7710

Editor: Arthur L. Zapel
Editorial Coordinator: Jennifer Vokolek McAloon
Cover and book design: Janice Melvin
Interior illustrations: Adrea Gibbs, Janice Melvin

Library of Congress Cataloging-in-Publication Data

Gibbs, Adrea, 1960-
    Let's put on a show! : a beginner's theatre handbook for young actors /
by Adrea Gibbs. -- 1st ed.
      p. cm.
   Includes index.
    SUMMARY: A guidebook for young would-be thespians, covering theatre vocabulary, scripting, casting, staging, sets and scenery, props, costumes, and makeup, as well as the basics of backstage and technical particulars.
   ISBN 1-56608-052-5 (pbk.)
   1. Theater -- Production and direction Juvenile literature. [1. Theater -- Production and direction.] I. Title.
   PN3157.G46 1999
   792'.023--dc21

                                      99-38372
                                         CIP

2   3   4   04 05 06 07

This book is dedicated to my mom and dad, Joe and Laureta Gibbs.

Dad, thanks for teaching me the importance of self-discipline, order, organization, good management, dependability, rationality, listening, how to drive and how to be driven, how to back up a trailer and stick-to-it-ness.

Mom, thanks for sharing your creativity with scissors and fabric, buttons and bows, cake frosting, glue and glitter, showing me how to laugh and cry, for being passionate, compassionate, and everything in between, with me.

It has been a blessing to be your daughter and share such a jubilant life with both of you and my wonderful brothers, Greg, Brian and Matthew. You have all invested so much belief in me and all my zaniness. This is but the tiniest of thank yous.

All my love,

My Special Thank Yous

I would be remiss if I did not thank those who have supported me throughout this exciting journey. Not only have I been a million miles away from home, but a million miles away from those I care most about who have lent their unending support and laughed, sometimes even guffawed, loudly, at my tales of the Mysterious East.

To (in no particular order as they are all performers and quite sensitive to their billing … ha, ha, ha!) Suzanne, Eric, Susan, Chuck, Mark and Elin who have been my ears and my sounding board. Were it not for e-mail, I think we would all be lost. Except for Chuck, who is a traditionalist and lives by the pen, not the keyboard. You are the best pals a gal could ever have and I thank you all for your kind and generous support and love.

To Reggie, who has always encouraged me to write and explore the vast world of the written word and often privy to my feeblest attempts. This is from my heart.

To my wonderful, crazy, and completely inspirational family … Mom and Dad, you are the greatest. Greg & Robin, Brian & Ellen, and Matt & Cass, the best siblings a big sister could ever have, by birth or marriage.

And last, … but not least, to my niece, Hunter, and my nephew, Mitchell, and all the other little ones to come. This is written with the hope that you, too, can learn to love and appreciate and find the theatre as magical and exciting as I have.

I Love You All

Adrea

Hey, Kids!

Have you ever wanted to put on your own show? A musical, maybe? Or a mystery? Something dramatic? How about doing a show with puppets? There are many different things you can do with lots of imagination and just a few things you can find around the house.

This book will also tell you about different parts of theatre and some of what goes into the creation of a professional production. Theatre even has its own special vocabulary; so when you see a word that is unfamiliar or for which you would like clarification, check the glossary at the back of the book.

There are lots of special tips and secrets (which an actor never divulges) in this book to guide you in the development of your own scripts, sets, costumes, special effects and more, using things that you can find around the house, at school or in the supermarket or drug store. These ideas are all shared to help make your show and experience creating a show fun from start to finish! So what do you say we get started and …

Let's Put On A Show!

Dear Parents, Teachers and Mentors,

Kids are filled with imagination. Given something as simple as the leftover cardboard from a roll of paper towels, they will find telescopes, flutes, swords and many things that neither you nor I would even begin to discover.

Exposure to the theatre is a tremendous way to enhance anyone's naturally creative spirit. Most kids, even the most shy, have a desire to perform once in a while, even if it is alone in front of a mirror. Many children who see actors on stage singing and dancing familiar, and not-so-familiar, stories find them breathtaking and inspiring. The lights. The costumes. The makeup. The music. It all blends together in a magical spectacle that speaks to the heart and soul of the child in us all.

Since long before Mickey Rooney and Judy Garland were saying, "Hey, kids! Let's put on a show!," there was someone who played the class clown or overly-dramatic actress. Whether they kept us laughing or rolling our eyes, we could appreciate, though often not consciously fully comprehend, the great value found in both being entertained and in entertaining.

Involvement in theatre also brings together many wonderful and exciting developmental experiences. In addition to offering kids the chance to explore their creativity in a variety of challenging applications, it can aid in developing self-confidence, poise, self-esteem, and, in learning to work with others, the gratification and special satisfaction of being a team member and striving toward a common goal.

What I hope I bring to both the adults and kids who have the opportunity to enjoy this book are some very basic tools for opening up an entire trunk-full of creative activities which can be done collectively to form a show or as individual projects.

Many things are not included in this book, in part for sheer lack of space. But the intent of its design is to be a springboard for the imagination and a starting point to introduce the wonders of theatre into a kid's life. Maybe even into your own.

With Best Wishes,

AdreaGibbs

Table of Contents

First Things First

Important Things to Remember

These are some IMPORTANT tips to think about, remember, and practice when you are planning on doing a show.

1. Please ask permission before borrowing, taking or using anything that does not belong to you. This includes: clothing, makeup, bed sheets, pillow cases, towels, kitchen supplies, glue, tape, scissors and any other supplies.

2. Please ask for help when you are planning on doing any heavy or difficult cutting or using hot glue. Some tools can be hard to handle and/or require two or more people to use correctly. *Remember, safety first.*

3. Please be polite. Good manners go a long way in accomplishing many things whether it is asking for assistance or permission to use something.

4. Please try to include everyone who would like to participate in the activity. It is a great way to make new friends.

5. Please let everyone share his or her ideas. Kids, even adults, have some really great ideas. You may be surprised!

6. Please clean up after you are done. Part of the magic of doing a show is that everything disappears when it is all over. Including the trash.

This may seem like a lot to think about, but it will make your show even better and more fun. These special hints are also great things to practice daily!

A Good Place to Start

The word **SHOW** means to display or present. In other words, to physically demonstrate by pretending, also known as play-acting, to express your ideas, thoughts, or stories through a theatrical means. Simply put, by acting out a story.

There are many words used to describe different kinds of shows. Some descriptive examples are **PLAY, MUSICAL, READING, PRODUCTION** or **PRESENTATION.** Not only are these labels descriptive, they also serve to identify and categorize more precisely what type of show an actor may be auditioning for or what an audience will be seeing.

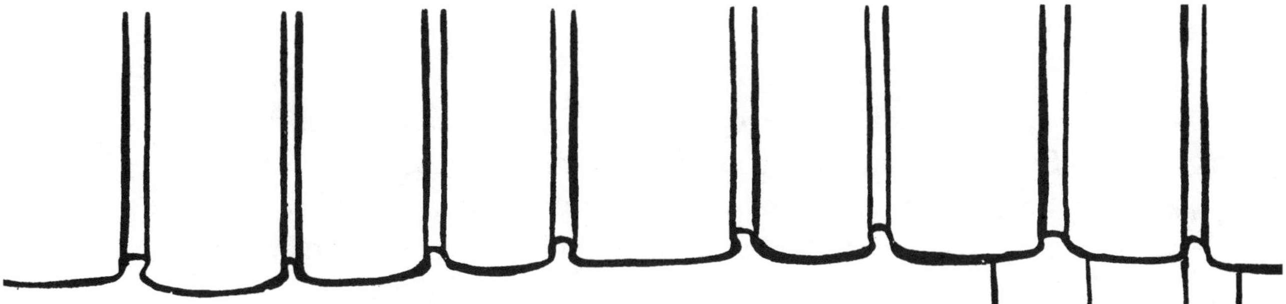

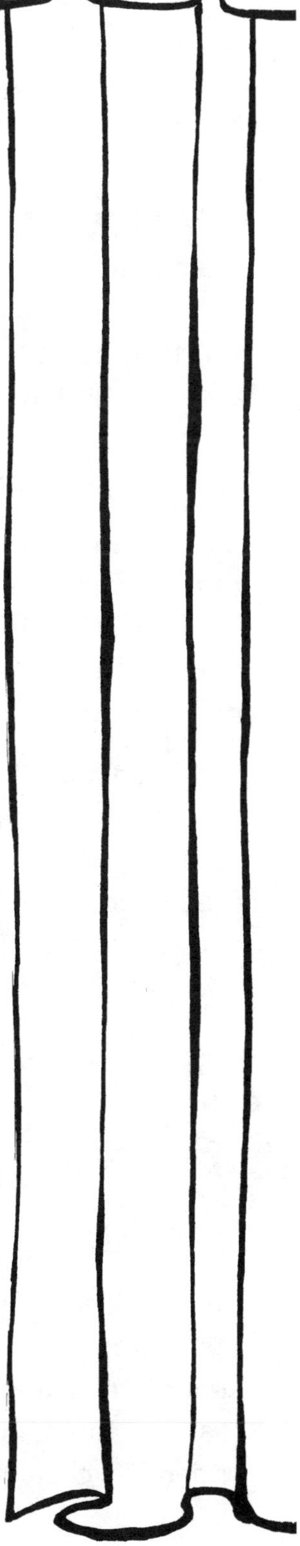

Once you begin to study different varieties of shows, you may be quite surprised at how many there are. Your greatest challenge may simply be in trying to choose exactly what kind you would like to do. Will you choose a drama? Or a comedy? Are you thinking about doing an ensemble show or would you prefer trying something solo? You must also decide if you will have rehearsals or prefer improvising.

To help you make a selection, let's take a look at some of these shows. You may want to choose a specific style for your production or possibly even try your idea using several different concepts.

VARIETIES OF SHOWS

DRAMA
COMEDY
PANTOMIME
IMPROVISATION
ONE-PERSON SHOW
MUSICAL
PUPPET SHOW
CIRCUS
READING

A **DRAMA** is a serious story. Dramas are usually associated with storylines that are heart rending or sad, often with moralistic overtones. Many are based on historical occurrences, folklore or fictional accounts. Several variations of the drama are suspense, mystery or horror genres. While these particular types maintain the serious elements attributed to dramas, serving to distinguish them from other types of productions, they further define the type of performance.

A **COMEDY** follows a humorous storyline. As with the drama, it could also be based on historical occurrences, folklore or fictional accounts. It may be written as a slapstick comedy filled with flying whipped cream pies or a silly melodrama where the audience becomes part of the action by hissing at the villains and cheering for the hero and heroine. A comedy is supposed to make the audience laugh!

Sometimes, the most difficult part about being an actor in a comedy (and sometimes in a drama, too, because you never know what may happen!) is not **BREAKING CHARACTER**. Breaking character means that you laugh or miss a line you are to speak because something has caught you off-guard and distracted you from your performance.

Virtually any kind of show can be either a drama or a comedy. In fact, it is quite common to see small bits of comedy used in drama, and vice versa, in order to achieve a dramatic effect. This type of technique has been employed since the earliest theatrical productions. In other words, by contrasting the styles, a dramatic moment used in comedy, for example, can add greater strength and more interest to a particular idea or thought.

A **PANTOMIME** is a play or skit that is done without the use of words. Occasionally set pieces, scenery and props are used, but traditional mimes, the name given to performers of pantomime, prefer to use only themselves to create their imagery. Everything is done by pretending and often requires a great amount of strength, agility, creativity and imagination on both the part of the audience and performer to make the illusion work. For example, if you wanted to sit down, you might act as though you were sitting on an imaginary chair and because you are able to make it look so realistic, the audience would understand and believe you were actually sitting in a chair. Marcel Marceau is considered the classic mime and is well known for his remarkable performances and traditional whiteface makeup, an identifying feature of mimes.

IMPROVISATION can be a great exercise for your brain and your body, because it requires you to create your performance instantaneously without rehearsal based upon circumstances presented for which you are not prepared. Many improvs utilize audience participation by having people suggest different types of characters and situations, challenging the performers to create a funny scene. Sometimes, when performing in a play or musical, an actor is required to use his or her improvisational skills if something unexpected happens, such as a fellow actor forgetting lines or a piece of scenery falling over or not working properly. Improvisation requires a great deal of spontaneity and the ability to observe and listen to fellow performers, all the while staying in character.

In a **ONE-PERSON** or **SOLO** show, one individual performs everything. Some of these shows are presented as a series of vignettes, skits or scenes that allow a performer to demonstrate a range of characters and emotions. Many shows of this type include singing and dancing or could be presented as one long speech called a **MONOLOG**. In a solo show, the performer can speak to either imaginary characters (in a sense, pantomiming their appearances on stage) or directly to the audience in a conversational manner. If the character (performer) is talking to him or herself, this specific type of monolog is called a **SOLILOQUY**, which allows a character to transmit his personal thoughts to an audience by thinking out loud.

A **PLAY** is a series of scenes that connect together to form a complete story. A **MUSICAL** is a play whose story is told through means of singing and dancing. Musicals use different kinds of music including jazz, pop, country, rock 'n' roll, folk and cultural songs. Musicals also use a variety of dance styles such as tap, modern, acrobatic, jazz and often incorporate popular dances from history like the Charleston, Jitterbug or the Funky Chicken. **OPERAS** are similar to musicals, except their stories are told primarily through classical music. **BALLET**, which is a formal style of dance, also uses modern and classical music but, traditionally, excludes the use of singing to relay the story, instead interpreting through movement.

PUPPET SHOWS can be performed with a great variety of puppets, each of which is classified by its particular characteristics. Marionettes are on strings with the puppeteer standing above the stage to manipulate or work the puppet. Hand puppets are worn on the hands, just as finger puppets are worn on the fingers. In these cases, the puppeteer is usually below or behind the stage and not visible to the audience. Stick puppets, shadow puppets, and full-sized (human-sized) puppets are also popular in puppet theatre. Puppetry is an extremely old form of theatre very popular around the world. Many cultures use puppet shows to tell fables, legends and stories with a moralistic teaching.

A traditional **CIRCUS** is performed in a ring under a tent, also known as the **BIG TOP**. Many include presentations done by daredevils, acrobats, high wire and trapeze artists, clowns and are led by an emcee called a **RINGMASTER**. Circuses also have a very long history around the world since they were traveling productions that could move from town to town and entertain the people. Today, while many circuses still appear in tents, others are performed on a stage or in sports arenas.

A **READING** sounds exactly like what it is. The actors sit or stand and read the lines of their characters directly from the pages of the script. Sometimes a playwright will have a reading as a way to see if his play makes sense and to make certain that all the pieces of the story fit together logically. There are also **STAGED READINGS**, sometimes called **READERS THEATRE**, where the actors still carry their scripts in order to read their lines. However they are also blocked by a director to show what sort of movement may take place during the actual performance.

There are many other varieties of performance that can be explored by going to the library, your local theatre, college or through websites on the Internet. These are also great resources for finding published plays or stories that you might be interested in presenting. In your research, you may discover that some shows follow very rigid format structures, while others appear to break all the rules by combining bits and pieces from many different theatrical styles. You may have your own idea for a show and choose to write the script yourself. Use your imagination!

Good Information

As was mentioned in the previous chapter, a play is performed by actors through the use of **DIALOG**. Dialog is the term used to describe the conversation between characters.

Writing your own play can be quite fun and definitely a challenge. To begin, you must come up with a **PLOT**. The plot is the story told in the play. Many writers like to use a story that is already familiar, such as a fairy tale, fiction-based or non-fiction-based story. If you choose to use material that is already in publication, you would then be basing your play on someone else's story. This is called an **ADAPTATION**. You can also create your own plot, making it an original story.

An important thing to remember about all plays and stories is that they must have a beginning, a middle and an ending.

Parts of a Play

A play is written in a special format or style called a **SCRIPT**. A script is made of up of many different parts which assist in the actual production of the play. Listed here are some of the main parts that will help you to understand the composition of a play.

A good **TITLE** is very important to your play and should give your cast, production team, and eventually the audience, an idea as to what the play is about. It should have some significant connection to the story such as the name of a character, a description of a particular setting or a reference to an event revealed during the play.

The **PLAYWRIGHT** is the author the play. Sometimes several people will collaborate (work together), so all the names would be listed. If you write your own show, you would then be a playwright.

AUTHOR = PLAYWRIGHT

If your play is created from a story that somebody else has written, then it is based upon, or adapted from, that story. You always want to credit (recognize or acknowledge) the person whose story gave you the idea for your play.

It is always a good idea to record the day, month and year you wrote your play. That way, in the future, when you write more plays, you will have an accounting of all your works and can remember your first efforts as a playwright!

Background Information

You will find this information in the beginning pages of most scripts and it is used to assist everyone who is working on the production to understand the premise behind the play. The director can use this information so he or she can determine how best to instruct and block the actors. The actors can learn something about the history of their characters so they can develop their character's personality, traits and idiosyncrasies (quirks). The set designer, costume designer and the many other designers involved can also decide how to create the physical aspects of the play to best suit the plot and the characters.

A **SYNOPSIS** gives a brief overview of the entire story quickly. It mentions the characters and important events related to those characters that create the conflict of the play.

TIME, in relation to a script, can refer to several different areas. When the events take place in the play is extremely important information.

CHRONOLOGICAL TIME refers to the morning, afternoon or evening as well as a specific hour of the day or night.

SEASONAL TIME refers to Spring, Summer, Fall or Winter.

HISTORICAL TIME identifies the time period in which the story happens such as the past, present or future.

Time can also change with every scene of the play.

Each kind of time is used to create a specific mood or atmosphere for the play. This information will help you to decide how physical elements of the show should look. This includes casting, costuming, the set, lighting and sound.

The **SETTING** is where the story takes place and could be anywhere such as a country, state, city, on another planet — even in a particular room in a house. Information about the setting will assist an actor in developing character traits and making certain choices such as whether or not to use an accent. Likewise, it will help the costume designer determine what costuming will be most suitable, the set designer create an appropriate set, as well as provide valuable information for other areas of the production. Settings, just as with time, can change with each new scene.

The **CAST OF CHARACTERS** is the listing of all the roles, or parts, in the play. Sometimes, additional information will be provided about each character such as physical traits (age, physical appearance, any special characteristics) particularly if those traits have significance in the storyline. There may also be descriptions of personality traits (sweet, good, evil, confused, forgetful) included and different relationships between characters such as parent, spouse, sibling, neighbor, enemy or friend.

You can see how every piece of information, even if it appears to be insignificant, will help when you are constructing a play. When you borrow a play from the library, see if you can locate the different areas that can supply background information for the story.

Characters, Directionals, Dialog and Other Stuff

Lines

When you write a play, it is through the characters' spoken **LINES** and directed actions that the story is told to the audience.

A line is a sentence a character speaks. An example of written lines might be like this:

HUNTER: I am so glad that Grandma and Grandpa brought us to the Pumpkin Patch. Have you ever seen so many pumpkins in all of your life?

MITCHELL: Never. I just hope that old headless horseman doesn't come around here. I may have to show him a thing or two, if he does.

HUNTER: Oh, forget about it. That's just some stupid superstition Uncle Gregory likes to scare everyone with.

When following a standard written format for a play, the character name is placed at the head of the line, usually in **CAPITAL LETTERS** and separated with a colon, so it stands apart from the dialog. Dialog occurs when two or more people have a conversation. By placing the character's name at the head of each line, the actors know who speaks which line and in what order the lines are spoken.

Directionals

A **DIRECTIONAL** is found inside parentheses following the character's name. It is different from the text by means of the type (like italics). One of the purposes for a directional is to suggest a particular type of movement or activity to be used in the staging. A directional can sometimes be as important as the dialog in order to make a scene work for the best

HUNTER: (*Crossing over to a giant pumpkin*) Hey, this one looks perfect for the contest!

MITCHELL: (*Crossing to join Hunter*) Wow! It's huge! How much do you think it weighs?

HUNTER: (*Trying to pick it up*) A lot. I think we are going to need some more help. Maybe you can find Grandma and Grandpa. They had a wheelbarrow.

MITCHELL: (*Running off stage*) GRANDMA! GRANDPA! We found the perfect one!

Another use of the directional can suggest a certain type of emotion to be used during a directional line. For example:

HUNTER: (*Very nervously*) Uh, oh. I think the pumpkin is slipping.

MITCHELL: (*Trying hard not to laugh*) I don't think we can hold onto it.

HUNTER: (*Surprised, as the pumpkin rolls away*) Oh, no!

MITCHELL: (*Laughing, as he chases the pumpkin*) GRANDPA! Stop that pumpkin!

An emotional directional is placed into a script to assist the director and actor in creating the proper mood for a scene.

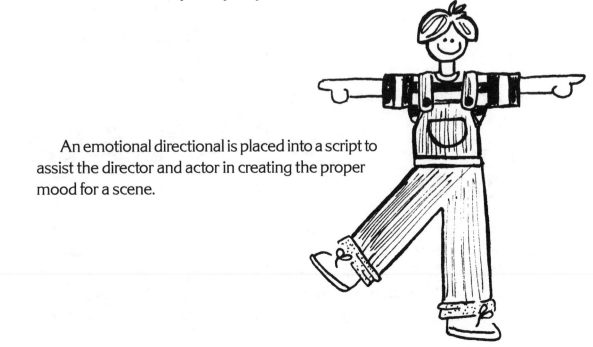

Not every line in a script requires a directional. For many playwrights, directionals serve to establish a foundation for a character, both emotionally and physically. Directionals cover everything from speech patterns and nervous habits to personality quirks. Most playwrights reserve their directionals so they can place emphasis into a scene when something pivotal to the plot occurs.

Sometimes, instead of writing a directional for individual lines, a short description of the action can be given setting up the action and emotional direction for the actors and director at the beginning of the scene. This description can explain what will be or has happened and how the characters may be feeling in response to the events. A description could run something like this …

HUNTER and MITCHELL have been visiting with their GRANDMA and GRANDPA. They are really excited because they are going to the pumpkin patch to pick out a pumpkin for the contest at school. They are a little nervous after hearing about the tale of the headless horseman who haunts there.

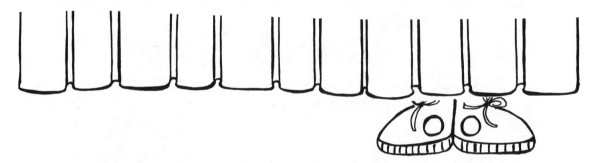

This background information will give valuable assistance to anyone who may want to perform your play.

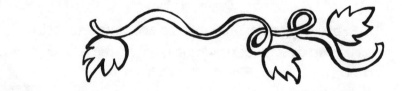

Scenes

Each section of a play is divided into **SCENES**. A scene is made up of a grouping of lines that occur during a particular part of the plot. For example, if your characters go to the pumpkin patch and buy a pumpkin, all the activity that happens at that time in the pumpkin patch could be Scene One (S.1, for short). Scene Two (S. 2) might be back at Grandma and Grandpa's house where the jack-o-lantern is carved for the contest. And Scene Three (S.3) could be at school where their jack-o-lantern wins first prize and the headless horseman shows up!

It is also important to note that scenes can also be separated by time, not just place, or by the changing of characters. If your story occurs at the same location for the duration of the play, scenes can be determined by time of day, week or year. If your scenes are changed based upon the action of the characters, such as when one character or several characters complete an interaction, a new scene can begin as those characters exit and different characters enter or through a combination of exiting, staying and entering. The determining factor to when a scene changes is traditionally based upon there being a different subject matter and/or focus from the previous scene.

One really long scene that has a beginning of a story, a middle, and ends with a silly joke, is called a **SKIT**.

When scenes are put together and performed in succession, they are collectively called an **ACT**. Your play can have one, two or even three acts. A One Act Play has the entire story, beginning, middle and end, told within a few scenes. In a full-length production, in which there are two or more acts, Act One (A.I., for short) introduces the plot and ends where some type of conflict or problem has arisen. The following act, Act Two (A.II), resolves the conflict or problem.

When distinguishing acts from the scenes when writing the plays, playwrights use a special numbering system. Traditionally, scenes are given Arabic Numerals, the numbers we use daily. Acts use Roman Numerals (letters from our alphabet). They were used by the ancient Romans in their system of counting.

ROMAN NUMERALS

Between the acts is an **INTERMISSION**. This pause allows both the actors and the audience to take a short break, stretch their legs, and maybe get something to eat or drink. It also provides an opportunity for the crew to make a set change and move any scenery required for the next act.

If you were going to draw a diagram of how a play is organized using all of the different parts of a script, it would look something like this:

ACT ONE

ACT I, SCENE 1
LINE:
LINE:

ACT I, SCENE 2
LINE:
LINE:

ACT I, SCENE 3
LINE:
LINE:

Did you notice that the numbers used for the ACTS and SCENES are not the same?

Roman numerals identify the ACTS.

INTERMISSION

ACT TWO

ACT II, SCENE 1
LINE:
LINE:

ACT II, SCENE 2
LINE:
LINE:

ACT II, SCENE 3
LINE:
LINE:

Arabic numerals identify the scenes. You might see something on a rehearsal schedule like A. I, SC.3. That means you would be rehearsing ACT ONE (I), SCENE 3.

THE END

How to Write Your Own Play

Here's a chance for you to try your hand at playwriting. Gather together your ideas and try them out here. These few pages will help you get started.

TITLE OF PLAY:

_____

(What you want to call your play)

WRITTEN BY:

_____

(Your name and the name of anyone else who helped you write the play)

BASED UPON A STORY BY:

_____

(If your play is from a story by someone else, you will want to include the title and the name of the original author. If the story is your own, one that you had previously written, you can place that information here, too.)

DATE PLAY WAS WRITTEN:

_____

(When did you write this play?)

CAST OF CHARACTERS:
(List all the different roles to be played and the descriptions of each.)

_____

_____

_____

_____

_____

THE PLOT:
(Give a synopsis of the story.)

_____

_____

_____

_____

_____

_____

_____

_____

_____

THE SETTING:

_____

(This is where your play takes place.)

THE TIME:

_____

(This is what time, the hour of the day, special date, or year your play takes place.)

BACKGROUND REGARDING ACTION THAT HAS PREVIOUSLY
TAKEN PLACE: _____
(Action that is relevant to the plot that has taken place prior to the opening
of the play or action that must be played prior to the dialog.)

_____

_____

_____

_____

_____

DIALOG: _____

(Your character's conversations and monologs that will relay your story to the audience. Remember to include important information such as directionals and make certain each character's line is identified with the character's name in capital letters.)

_____

_____

_____

_____

_____

_____

_____

_____

_____

_____

_____

_____

_____

_____

_____

_____

_____

_____

The End

If you need more pages for your play, use a notebook or pieces of paper you can put into a binder or folder. It will make it easier for you to work on and edit. General things to think about when you are working on your play: character names, movement and any change of setting or time that may be important to the development of your plot.

Finding a Place to Perform

Now that you have decided what kind of performance you would like to do, whether it may be a play, musical or a one-person show, you might want to think about where you would like to hold your performance.

Most people think of a show as being on a **STAGE**. Stages are traditionally thought of as being an area with a raised floor and a curtain which closes between scenes and acts so the crew can move set pieces and the actors can get into their places without being seen by the audience.

If you would like to use someplace with a traditional stage area, check your school, church, synagogue, temple or library. Ask about how to book (make reservations) to use the stage for your performance.

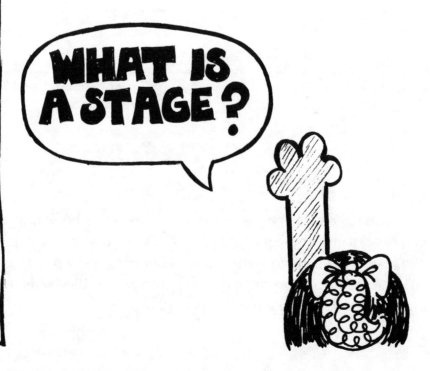

WHAT IS A STAGE?

The Stage

A stage is made of lots of parts and each has a special name.

The **FLY SPACE** is up by the ceiling. The fly (for short) is where some of the scenery, usually backdrops, can be kept. The scenery is flown in (that means dropped down from the ceiling and into position on the stage) and helps to create different scenes for the play. In other words, the scenery flies in and out, kind of like a bird.

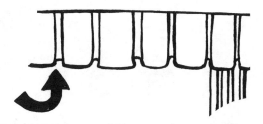

The **WINGS** are the sides of the stage. Actors will often wait in the wings before making their entrances. They can also leave the stage through the wings when making their exits. The long curtains that hang in the wings are called **LEGS** and help to cover the exits and entrances. Legs may be named so because they look a bit like a pair of long pants!

The **CURTAIN** separates the audience from the performance and hangs in front of the stage. Some plays do not use the curtains. In fact, sometimes the actors come right out into the audience. This is called **BREAKING THE FOURTH WALL** because, normally, the audience is watching the play as if the wall to the house they are looking through is invisible. In fact, the place where the audience sits is called the **HOUSE!**

The stage is also the floor area and can also be called the **DECK** or **FLOORBOARDS**. A stage is divided up into different imaginary areas so the director can tell the actors exactly where they should go during the blocking. This diagram is as if you were looking down at the stage floor from the **FLY GALLERY** (the ceiling).

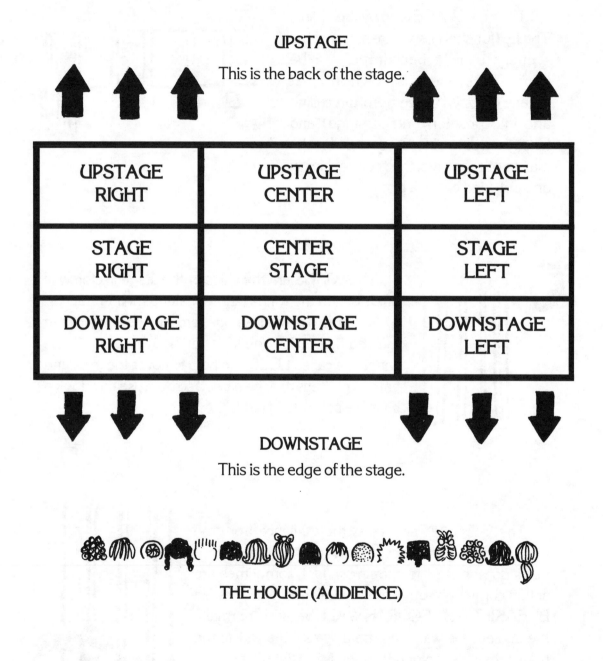

UPSTAGE

This is the back of the stage.

UPSTAGE RIGHT	UPSTAGE CENTER	UPSTAGE LEFT
STAGE RIGHT	CENTER STAGE	STAGE LEFT
DOWNSTAGE RIGHT	DOWNSTAGE CENTER	DOWNSTAGE LEFT

DOWNSTAGE

This is the edge of the stage.

THE HOUSE (AUDIENCE)

Interesting Information

When you are standing on stage, instead of saying you are standing at the front of the stage or at the back of the stage, you would say you are **DOWNSTAGE** (meaning at the front of stage closest to the audience) or **UPSTAGE** (meaning you are standing at the back of the stage).

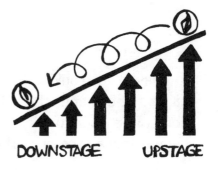

DOWNSTAGE   UPSTAGE

The terms upstage and downstage originated a very long time ago, when the stages of theatres were built on a **RAKED STAGE**. A raked stage means the stage is slanted, the back higher and the front lower. Stages were built this way so that the audience, particularly the people who stood on the ground closest to the stage, could see the action on the stage better. These audience members were called **GROUNDLINGS**.

So, in the early days of theatre, when a director asked an actor to go upstage, he was asking the actor to go to the highest part (the back) of the stage or, if asked to go downstage, to the lowest part (the front) of the stage. A simple way to remember these terms is like this: if you walked to the back of a raked stage and placed a marble there, the marble would roll from upstage to downstage and right into the audience. Though most stages today are flat, the names are still used as a means to give direction.

It is not always necessary to perform on a traditional stage with a raised floor and a curtain. In fact, if you use your imagination and creativity, you can set your performance just about anywhere. Here are some different ideas:

How about using a closet? You could even use the clothes on the hangers as an impromptu curtain. There may not be enough room to fit an entire cast inside, but it could be just the right size for a solo act or a puppet show.

Maybe you could use a garage and hang a sheet from the open garage door to be your curtain. Or close the garage door and use it as a backdrop.

Try stringing a clothesline across the yard or inside the house (which is great on rainy days). This makes a terrific place to hang sheets for your curtain.

You could try throwing a sheet, blanket or cloth over a table and present your show from underneath it. This works really well for puppet shows.

Another good option for puppet shows would be to place a table on its side. This set-up can be used with hand or finger puppets or marionettes which require the puppeteer to be standing over the puppet to manipulate it.

The next time you are at the grocery store, ask the store manager if he or she may have a large box you could have. Cut straight down one side, open up the box and you can have another great place to do a puppet show.

Or turn the box upside-down and cut a big window in the front of it and place it on top of a table. Be sure to slide the box far enough back from the edge of the table so you can easily move your arm around inside.

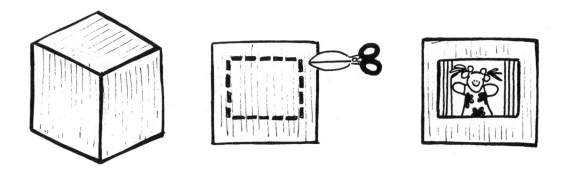

What other non-traditional areas can you think of as possible performance venues? Outdoors, trees and bushes can be used to create staging areas or a fountain can be used as a backdrop. See how creative you can be in finding a place for your show.

If you are thinking about producing a show, you should also consider that not every production needs to have a curtain. In fact, some theatres are designed in interesting shapes and configurations that would make it difficult to use a curtain at all.

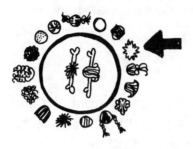

One particular kind of stage that is used is **IN-THE-ROUND.** The name refers to the fact that the audience is seated all the way around the stage area and actors for the performance.

Another type is a **THRUST STAGE.** Sometimes a thrust stage will use a curtain across the **PROSCENIUM,** or main part of the stage. However, the majority of the performance takes place on the area that protrudes out into the house where the audience is seated around three sides to watch.

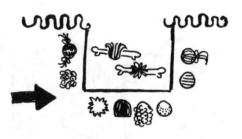

Street performers, such as mimes, magicians and some acting troupes, use sidewalks, streets and courtyards (open spaces) of malls and shopping centers to entertain. That is one of the many things that makes theatre so exciting. It is also one of the reasons why theatre has been around for centuries. You can create a performance just about anywhere. All you need is your imagination.

William Shakespeare, a very famous playwright, wrote a line in *As You Like It* that says, "All the world's a stage …" and, as you can see, he was right!

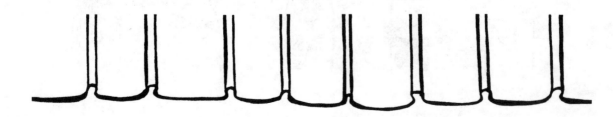

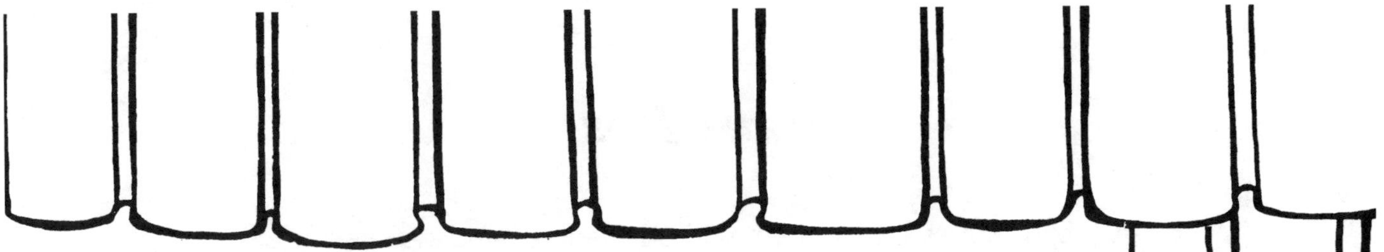

Making the Show Work

There are lots of people who help to create a production. In professional theatre, there are many specialized jobs.

To name but a few of them:

DIRECTOR
ASSISTANT DIRECTOR
CHOREOGRAPHER
MUSICAL DIRECTOR
CONDUCTOR
SET DESIGNER
LIGHTING DESIGNER
AUDIO DESIGNER
STAGE MANAGER
COSTUME DESIGNER
MAKEUP & WIG DESIGNER
ORCHESTRA
CAST
STAGE CREW

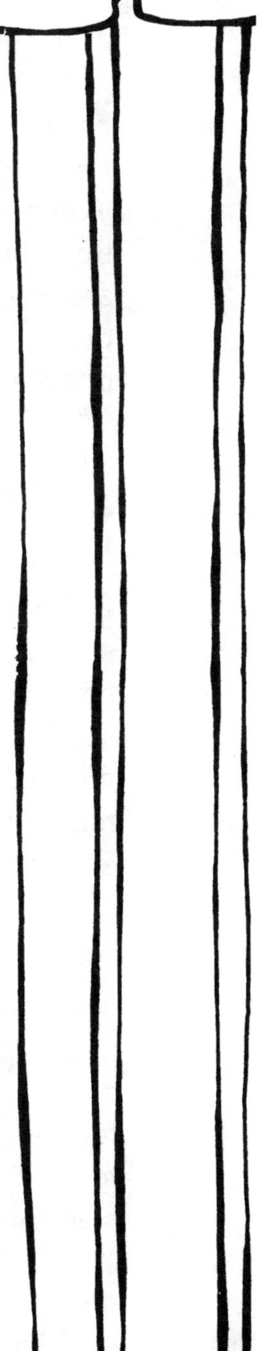

WHO HELPS TO PUT ON A SHOW?

Theatre Jobs

Every job in theatre is important. Without people handling specific parts of the show, such as lighting, special effects, box office transactions and costuming, for example, it could be very difficult to coordinate an entire production. Once everyone has read the script, the **PRODUCTION TEAM** works together to determine how best to put the show together. Everything from the plot to the characters to special requirements dictated in the script are discussed and considered. By bringing together the heads of each department, the show can be coordinated through group effort and positions clarified in order to achieve the most efficient team effort.

DIRECTOR

This is the artistic leader of entire production. The **DIRECTOR** runs rehearsals, decides how to block the actors, and works with all of the other members of the production team. The director sometimes has other jobs such as creating the choreography, designing the set or being the musical director. The director has a great responsibility to make certain that all areas of the production are coordinated and organized.

ASSISTANT DIRECTOR

The **ASSISTANT DIRECTOR**, or **A.D.** as it is sometimes called, helps the director to run rehearsals for the show, organize schedules and followup with the other departments to see that their goals are being met. Sometimes, the A.D. also acts as the stage manager for the production.

STAGE MANAGER

The **STAGE MANAGER** is responsible in making certain that the cast and crew are aware of their rehearsal schedule, keeps everything running on time, gives the cast breaks and makes sure performers are in their places when the show begins. He also calls the show. That means that he gives the lighting crew, the sound crew, and the stage crew their **CUES** during the performance so everyone knows when to do their particular job during the show. This is extremely important for the safety of everyone.

MUSICAL DIRECTOR / CONDUCTOR

The **MUSICAL DIRECTOR** teaches the music and lyrics to the cast and determines what part each performer will sing. There are four main voice pitches that are used in musicals, soprano (the high women's part), alto (the low women's part), tenor (the high men's part), and bass (the low men's part). Often, each part will sing a different melody. The M.D. (for short) will also teach the **SCORE** to the orchestra. The score is what the musical text is called for a show. Sometimes, the M.D. also acts as the **CONDUCTOR** leading the orchestra and cast through the music during the performance.

ORCHESTRA

The **ORCHESTRA** is made up of people who play musical instruments for the performance. The conductor leads both the orchestra and the cast in all of the musical numbers. Some musicals do not require a complete orchestra with string section (violins, violas, cellos and stringed basses), so often a band is used, requiring fewer musicians. Other musicals require very few instruments for the score and simply use a piano and drums.

SOUND DESIGNER

The **SOUND DESIGNER** creates the sound for the show. Microphones are a major part of the sound system. Body-mic, hand held, stand, floor and suspended microphones are several different choices. The sound designer also chooses monitors, speakers and mixing boards. Once all the equipment has been selected, using a mixing board, the sound designer will balance the sound of the cast while they are rehearsing. The sound coming through the microphones and a sound track or orchestra will be blended together on the mixing board so all the voices and instruments can be heard.

SET DESIGNER

The **SET DESIGNER** creates the drawings that show the rest of the production team what the set for the show will look like. It is the blueprint for the **CONSTRUCTION CREW**, the team that will build the set according to the specs (short for specifics). The set designer will use background information and the script to help determine what the appropriate setting will be so it is suitable to the needs of the play and the production team. It may be outdoors and have trees and bushes or indoors and require furnishings. The set designer will also work very closely with the lighting designer.

LIGHTING DESIGNER

The **LIGHTING DESIGNER** must figure out where all the lights must be placed above the stage in the rigging and above where the audience sits in the house. After the lighting plot is made, the lights will be hung on the grid. As the cast is rehearsing on stage, usually during Tech-Week, the lighting designer and lighting crew will begin to focus the lights for the show. This allows the audience greater visibility of the performers and will also add to the overall effect and mood of the show. The lighting designer will also add gels, gobos and other lighting effects, such as strobe lights and black lights, to further create the illusion.

STAGE CREW

The **STAGE CREW** is made up of all the people involved with the technical aspects of the theatre. The lighting crew hangs and takes care of all the lights and lighting effects. The sound crew deals with the sound (audio) equipment like the microphones, speakers and monitors. The wardrobe crew is in charge of all the costumes and costume repairs. The makeup and wig crews help the actors with their makeup and wigs. The people who work on the stage are called the deck or running crew because they often have to move very quickly during the show to make all of their cues. And all of the crews together are called the stage crew.

CHOREOGRAPHER

This person creates all the dances or staging for a musical. The **CHOREOGRAPHER** listens to the music for the show and decides what type of steps, or choreography, to do.  Then, the routines are taught to the cast. Sometimes the choreographer will also stage some of the physical action in the show such as a fight scene.

COSTUME DESIGNER

The **COSTUME DESIGNER** creates the designs for all the costumes (clothes) to be worn by the cast. The costumer (another name for the designer) also pays special attention to the details of the script, set design, lighting and overall artistic direction to assure the costuming is appropriate. Once finalized, the costume designer and the **WARDROBE CREW** create patterns or find existing costume pieces and construct (cut out and sew) the costumes for the show and make certain that all the costumes fit appropriately.

MAKEUP AND WIG DESIGNER

The **MAKEUP AND WIG DESIGNER** can be the same person or two different people. They work very closely with the costume designer to make sure that everybody in the cast has the right kind of hair and the right kind of makeup suitable to the character they are portraying. Often they train the actors how to put on their own wigs, apply specialty makeup and how to use special effects makeup, such as blood, for the greatest effect.

CAST

All of the **ACTORS** in a show are called the **CAST**. The individual parts or roles can also go by many different names. **PRINCIPALS**, or leads, which are also sometimes called leading men and leading ladies, are the stars of the show. They are the characters central to the plot. **SUPPORTING PLAYERS**, or supporting leads, normally have the second most lines or songs in the show and are the focus of the secondary plot or subplot. Featured players

usually have a special scene or number (song) in the show and sometimes play into the main plot or subplot. **ENSEMBLE PLAYERS** are utilitarian, playing lots of smaller roles. In the case of a musical, these performers are called the **CHORUS**, singing and dancing in most of the big musical production numbers. **UNDERSTUDIES** learn all of the principal, supporting and featured roles and go on stage if someone is on vacation, injured or ill. **SWINGS** do the same thing as understudies, but instead concentrate on learning all the chorus or ensemble roles.

As you can see, sometimes a lot of people are involved in creating a successful production and each one is an important part of the team. You won't need that many people to stage your own show, but everyone can **WEAR LOTS OF HATS** (do several different jobs). The best part is that everybody helps out doing whatever he or she can and it is a great team effort!

Now that we know a little about some of the people who help to put together a production, let's take a look at some of the technical aspects of the show.

Technical Theatre
Lighting, Special Effects and More

Technical theatre is all about what happens behind the scenes and includes all of the things that go on to make a show work, such as lighting and sound. Some shows have very complicated electrical and sound systems. Others are very simple. Below are examples of a few fancier technical effects you may see happen in a professional show.

Some professional shows have a system that uses the power of water to move heavy set pieces called **HYDRAULICS**. Hydraulic systems have made houses fly up in the air, giant tires float like flying saucers, and can even lower a specially designed stage to look like a cliff! What makes this illusion work is the audience cannot see the hydraulics operating because they are carefully designed, often hidden right in the scenery!

Other shows have special **AUDIO SYSTEMS**. Audio means sound, so the audio (sound) system would include microphones, speakers and monitors. There is also a specially designed audio system, the infrared sound system, created to help people who have difficulty hearing. It works by using special sound waves in the air.

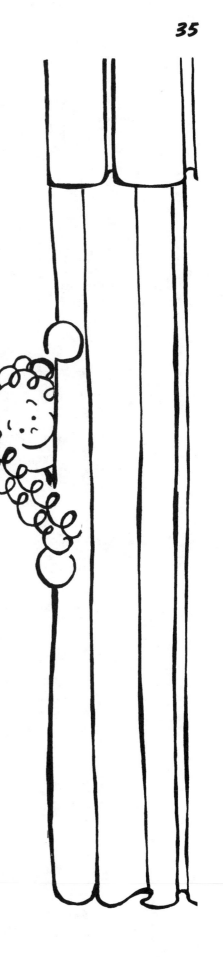

Many professional productions use different tricks to make the lighting interesting and unusual. **GOBOS** are one trick many lighting designers use. Gobos are special designs that are placed over the lights and create special shapes and effects on the stage and actors. **GELS** are a thin sheet of transparent (see through) color material that can be placed over a light to produce colored effects. Some shows use projected images, like movies and slides, or big screen televisions for added interest.

Special effects are also done with smoke, fog, fire and fireworks (pyrotechnics). These have to be done very carefully so the special effect is exciting, but even more importantly, so nobody gets hurt. Safety is always the single most important thing to be concerned with when putting on a show, especially when using any special effects.

How to Do Some of Your Own Technical Things!
Simple things you can try for your own show

AUDIO (SOUND)

If you do your show or play at a place that already has a stage (such as your school, library or place of worship), there may be a sound system available to you. Be certain to ask someone associated with the facility for assistance in operating the system properly. They may even be able to show you how to do it on your own.

Some people have boombox radios which can be attached to a microphone. This can be nice to use especially if you are doing a musical or are planning on using background music. You can also use a tape recorder and make your own recordings for special effects sounds like ghosts, footsteps or creaky doors.

In your production, you may not need to use a sound system. In theatre, actors are trained to speak loudly and clearly. This is called **PROJECTION**, because you project your voice out toward the audience. To illustrate this concept, imagine what the size is of a photographic slide. When the slide is placed into the slide projector, everyone can easily see what is on the slide. That is exactly the same way you must think about using your voice, as if you were putting it through a special voice magnifier.

Projection can be very tricky. Even though you are speaking loudly, it must also sound as though you are holding a conversation at what would be a normal volume level. That also means that if you need to yell, you must be a lot louder than normal. If you are telling another actor on stage a secret, you would use a **STAGE WHISPER**, a whisper that the audience can hear, in other words, a loud whisper. As an actor, you must learn to adjust your voice to being either much louder for yelling, or softer for whispering, but always remembering the audience needs to hear what is being said to follow the plot. Not only is consistent volume important, but so is the clear **ENUNCIATION** (the sounding out of all consonants and vowels) of your words.

VISUAL

If you are going to use a stage at your school, library or place of worship, there may already be some lights you can use. Ask someone associated with the facility to assist you with the lights. They will be able to show you what different types of lights you will have available to you and possibly even be able to instruct you in some simple light settings that could represent day or night time. You may even have access to gels. Remember a gel is a thin sheet of colored plastic used to make the stage different colors.

STAGE LIGHTS are hung from a grid located in the ceiling in order to light the majority of the stage efficiently. They can also be placed across the front of the stage as footlights, or stand in the wings clamped on to special poles called **TREES**. The placement of the lighting is charted (laid out) on a **PLOT PLAN** by the lighting designer and hung by the lighting crew.

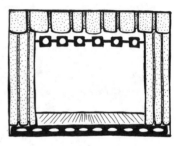

One type of specialty light is called a **STROBE LIGHT**. Another is a **BLACK LIGHT**. Strobe lights flash on and off very quickly and make the action on stage appear to be moving in slow motion. Black lights illuminate light colors making them glow, particularly fluorescent and neon shades. Black lights also make white appear to be purple and are often used in haunted houses to add spooky special effects.

If you are considering doing your show outside during the day, you probably won't have to concern yourself too much with lighting, because the sun will give you plenty. You may want to create some shade so it doesn't get too hot or bright for either your actors or audience. You can do this by using umbrellas, trees or by tying a blanket or sheet to poles or trees and stretching them overhead. To create some interesting designs using the sunlight and shadow, you could make shadow puppets or cut-outs that act like gobos and decorate the ground and stage with shadows and light shapes.

If you are doing your show inside and do not have access to regular stage lighting, you can creatively use the lights in the room or garage. You may want to try turning off the lights between scenes to indicate changes. If you would like to create a spotlight, try using a large flashlight. You could even provide for or ask your audience to bring along their own flashlights to help light your stage, which would make your production interactive!

How to Do Some Lighting Effects

Lighting effects will add variety to the lights you use in your production. Even if you are doing your show outside during the day, creating gobos, shadow puppets, and gels will add something special.

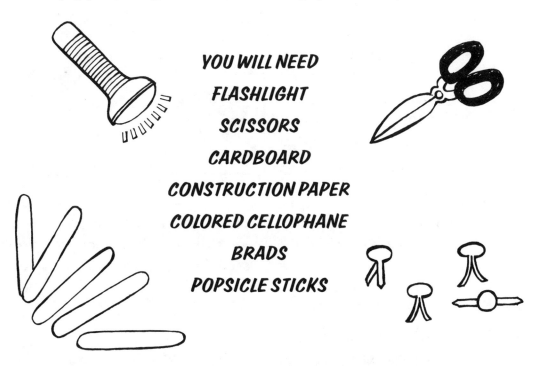

YOU WILL NEED

FLASHLIGHT

SCISSORS

CARDBOARD

CONSTRUCTION PAPER

COLORED CELLOPHANE

BRADS

POPSICLE STICKS

As you become more involved in theatre, you may want to experiment with new materials and create new and different lighting effects.

How to Make . . .

GOBOS

You can make large or medium-sized gobos that can be hung up or attached to a stick or post. Then the light or sun will shine through it to create your patterned design.

1. Choose a piece of cardboard and draw a design for your gobo.

2. Carefully cut out the shape, remembering that it is the cutout portion of the cardboard that will become your design in the light.

3. If you choose to hang it up, punch a hole at the top of your gobo and run string through it. You can also use a needle and thread.

4. If you would like to place it in the ground or attach it to a part of the set, you can add a popsicle stick, broomstick or yardstick, for example, to achieve the correct height and placement for your gobo pattern.

OR … you can make a little gobo and tape it to the front of a flashlight to create a mobile version.

SHADOW PUPPETS

1. Select a piece of cardboard and draw your puppet design.

2. Carefully cut out your design. With shadow puppets, the solid part of your design creates the pattern, the opposite way the light is used in gobos.

3. Tape or glue an appropriate length stick to the cardboard shape. Make certain that the stick is placed so it will not distract from the intended design.

4. Hang up a clothesline and fasten a light colored sheet across it. Hold your puppet up at what will be the backside of the sheet, furthest from the audience. Point a flashlight at the back of the sheet from behind the puppet so the shadow is created on the front.

SAFETY TIP: You should never attach anything, including tape, directly to a lightbulb or anything that is hot. Always attach to metal, wood or plastic.

GELS

1. Draw a frame for your gel on a piece of cardboard. Be certain that the frame is larger than the light you are planning on having colored so the edge of the frame will not hide any of your light. If you would like a special shape that will edge the colored light, again, you must see how large your light is and make the frame in a size that will allow the edge to be seen, similar to a gobo.

2. Cut out your frame.

3. Place your frame on colored cellophane and cut a piece out that is a little larger than the hole in your frame.

4. Tape the cellophane to the frame.

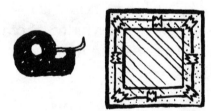

5. Attach, hang or place on a stick to use.

Now that you have some basic ideas, imagine what you could do using several flashlights from different angles or combining shadow puppets, gobos and gels.

How to Make Your Own Special Effects

Special effects can be a lot of fun to create for use in your show. Most of these things are very simple to do at home. Always make certain you are working in an open, well-ventilated area, that you have someone who can help you, and you have received proper permission. As with everything, safety is a priority.

YOU WILL NEED:

STYROFOAM PEANUTS
COTTON BALLS
LARGE BASKET
PLASTIC BUCKET
DRY ICE
FAN
WATERING CAN
FLASHLIGHT
RED and YELLOW CELLOPHANE
TINFOIL
LARGE PIECE OF CARDBOARD
BLACK PAINT
CONSTRUCTION PAPER
CLEAR PACKAGE TAPE
PAPER TOWEL ROLLS
TOILET PAPER ROLLS
LITTLE CHRISTMAS TREE LIGHTS

SUGGESTION: You may want to keep all of your special effects equipment together in the same place. Use a large box for storage so everything can be found easily for your next production or for when you are ready to experiment with some new effects!

How to Make...
Snow

1. Collect some Styrofoam peanuts, such as you will find in packing cartons, or cut up a lot of white paper into small bits.

2. Fill up a basket with your materials. The fuller the better.

3. Stand up on a secured ladder or chair high enough that you will be above where you want the snow to fall, but remain unseen by the audience. This may require some masking (covering) in the form of set pieces, traveler curtains or a dark crew uniform. When safely in position, gently shake the basket to create snowfall.

4. The snow can also be used to decorate the set by gluing it to pieces of the set or sprinkling it over the floor to create a snow-like effect.

Fog

1. Have an adult assist you in obtaining some dry ice. Be certain to use rubber gloves AT ALL TIMES when dealing with dry ice because it will burn you if not handled properly.

2. Fill up a bucket with water and carefully place it into position when effect will occur.

3. Carefully drop the ice into the bucket just prior to when you need the effect created.

4. Once you have dropped in the dry ice. The water will start to bubble. Fog will appear. Use a fan to move the fog in the direction you need.

5. Be certain to STRIKE (remove) all of your fog effects materials immediately following the special effect.

Rain

1. Fill a watering can with water. Make certain you do not fill your can so full that you cannot easily control it.

2. Set up a bucket below where you will be sprinkling the water.

3. Stand on a chair or ladder and sprinkle the water. You may want to try several different types of watering cans to see which one will create the right type of effect you are seeking.

SAFETY TIP: Always make certain that your chair or ladder is secured either to the wall or with someone assisting you by holding it in position.

Stars

1. Select a piece of cardboard large enough to create your star effect. Mark where you would like to place your stars.

2. Using the point of a pair of scissors, carefully poke holes where you have made all your marks. They will need to be large enough for the small lightbulbs to securely fit through.

3. Paint the cardboard black or dark blue.

4. Gently push mini yellow or white Christmas lights through the holes.

SAFETY TIP: Make certain that your cord is long enough to reach an outlet and it can be placed out of the way so no one will get caught in it or trip on it.

Fire

1. Paint toilet paper and/or paper towel rolls to look like wood. Let dry.

2. Draw a large flame and a half-circle on a piece of cardboard. Cut both pieces out.

3. Paint or color flame to look like fire. Let dry.

4. Cut out a piece of tinfoil in the shape of a flame and glue to the center of the painted flame.

5. Cut a short slit in the bottom of the flame and a slit of the same length in the top of the half-circle. Slide the two pieces together so the flame can stand on its own.

6. Surround standing flame with painted rolls.

7. For added effect, cover a flashlight with colored cellophane and flicker the flashlight beam back and forth across the tinfoil.

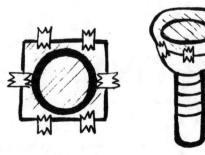

Earthquake

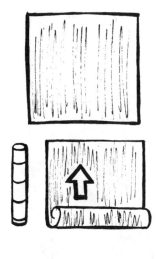

1. Get a large piece of cardboard. Check with the manager of your local grocery or department store and see if there is a large carton you may have. Refrigerator, stove and food carton boxes are great. You want to make certain that you can either piece together the cardboard or find a piece large enough to accommodate the set pieces and items you want to have effected by your earthquake.

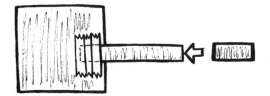

2. Locate a long cardboard tube, such as from wrapping paper, or create your own by rolling a piece of cardboard and taping it into a tube.

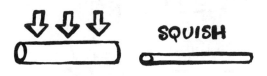

3. Squish the tube flat.

4. Attach the tube to the underside of your cardboard piece. Your tube needs to be long enough that the person who is creating the earthquake is completely off-stage and unseen by the audience. To add more length, use additional tubes.

5. Place your "earthquake" items on the cardboard and shake on cue. Make certain that your items are not too heavy and that they are non-breakable to make the effect work best and most safely. If you need a larger area covered by your cardboard, you may want to consider making several cardboard areas to be operated by different crew members. If you have actors who are caught in the earthquake, they can assist in creating the complete effect by standing off of the cardboard area and moving themselves about as if in the earthquake as well.

Wind

1. Collect several large pieces of cardboard.

2. Hold the cardboard against your body with your thumbs on top and fingers underneath next to your legs.

3. Using your entire arm, move the cardboard up and down. The faster you move, the more wind you will create. Try several crew members standing shoulder to shoulder and see if you can work up a tornado!

4. If you only require a small puff of wind or light breeze, such as would move window curtains or blow over a cup, try using a cardboard tube and directing it at the object. Then give a quick blow through the tube.

Using some of these ideas, what other special effects can you create?

From Wallpaper to Trees

What is a **SET**? The word set is the root (main part) of the word **SETTING**. The setting is the location, surroundings, and/or timing in which your play happens. The set is the collection of the different pieces that help to create the particular setting you are trying to achieve. This includes all set pieces such as sofas, chairs or tables, and location elements that might be represented by backdrops or flats. In other words, anything that physically suggests where and when the story is taking place.

Just like the setting, the different scenes in a play, or possibly each act, occur at a certain time and place and are reflected in the set design. The **SCENERY**, which is taken from the word scene, is another word used when discussing the set and usually refers to painted backdrops that show outdoor landscapes.

The set helps your audience and performers to experience and better visualize where the play is taking place.

A set does not need to be fancy in order to create the proper setting. Sometimes, it is far more effective when it is minimal. Most often items are borrowed, such as chairs and tables, with care being given to return them in good condition following your production.

When you are beginning to design your set, you should make certain that it is the right setting for your show. For example, if you are doing a period piece set in medieval times, it would be inappropriate to include electrical lamps as part of the set. You must also decide if you will be using a backdrop, flats and/or set pieces and how they will all work together to create the entire environment for the show.

How to Create Your Own Sets

You can have fun designing and building your own sets from backdrops to flats to set pieces! Here are some supplies you may want to gather in preparation.

CARDBOARD
CONSTRUCTION PAPER
SCISSORS
TISSUE PAPER
PENCIL
WRAPPING PAPER
NON-TOXIC POSTER PAINT
PAINT BRUSHES
PERMANENT MARKING PENS
HOLE PUNCHER
NEWSPAPER
PAPER TOWELS
CLOTHESLINE or STRING
CLOTHESPINS
OLD LARGE SHIRT
OLD SHEETS
WHITE GLUE
GLITTER
MASKING TAPE
CLEAR PACKAGE TAPE
EGG CARTONS
PLASTIC MARGARINE TUB

Look around to see what other materials you can discover that might be useful when designing and constructing your set, particularly recyclables!

These next items may be a little harder to come by, so see if you can find an adult to help you obtain and use the items listed below:

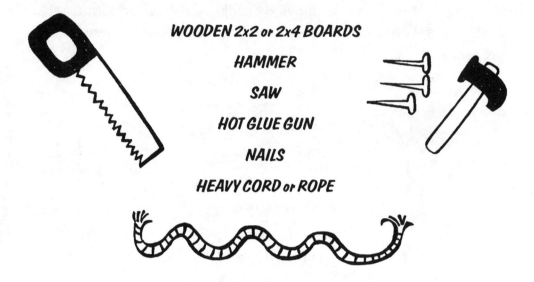

WOODEN 2x2 or 2x4 BOARDS

HAMMER

SAW

HOT GLUE GUN

NAILS

HEAVY CORD or ROPE

Here are some set pieces you may be able to borrow for your production:

A CARD TABLE

FOLDING CHAIRS

STEP LADDERS

PIECES OF LUMBER (WOOD)

STOOLS

BENCHES

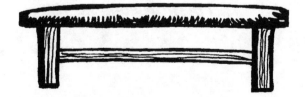

These are just a few suggestions to get you started.

How to Make a Backdrop

A **BACKDROP** is a large piece of fabric or cloth that is hung across the upstage area (the part of the stage furthest from the audience) from the fly (the ceiling).

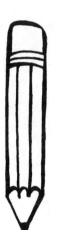

YOU WILL NEED

AN OLD SHEET or CARDBOARD

MASKING TAPE

A PENCIL

MARKING PENS or PAINTS and PAINT BRUSHES

PLASTIC MARGARINE TUB FILLED WITH WATER

PAPER TOWELS

OLD LARGE SHIRT

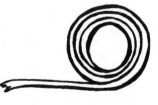

1. You may want to put on an old, large shirt to keep your own clothing clean or wear some old, comfortable clothing.

2. Pick a large, dry area to create your backdrop, preferably where there is not a lot of foot traffic. Your backdrop will need time to dry, maybe even overnight, so be certain you take that into consideration, as well.

3. Lay out all of your supplies and double-check that you have everything necessary before getting started. There is nothing worse that being halfway through a project and discovering you forgot to bring out something you need!

4. Lay out a sheet or taped together cardboard flat (make certain the taped side is turned down). Using a pencil, draw your background design. Remember to carefully consider what type of scenery will work best for your show because it will tell your audience a little something about where the story is taking place. It may be created to look like the inside of a living room (wallpaper, pictures, maybe a door), desert of cacti, dark jungle or perhaps a cityscape, like the skyline of New York City. It could even be a solid color or be decorated with the title of your show on it. There are many possibilities.

5. Once you are pleased with your sketch, you can begin to paint. You may want to first outline in permanent marking pen to help make your main design stand out. Use permanent marking pens if possible, because they will not run or smear into the other colors of your design.

6. Let your backdrop dry completely.

7. TOUCH-UP (fix or re-paint) any areas that need it. Let it dry again.

8. Hang the clothesline across at the point furthest upstage from your audience. Make sure that you tie the ends of the clothesline tightly and that it is tied to something that will not break or pull.

9. Using clothespins, hang the backdrop from the clothesline. After you have closed (finished) your show, you may want to save your backdrop for a future performance! If you are using a garage, you could also use masking tape to attach your backdrop directly to the door.

The backdrop can add a lot to your set and performance and it is a great piece of scenery.

How to Build a Flat

A **FLAT**, just like a backdrop, is also a traditional set piece. If several flats are attached together they can also act as a backdrop or be used for doors, walls, staircases and just about anything else you can think of that would add to your set.

YOU WILL NEED

FOUR-2X2 or 2X4 LUMBER BOARDS CUT TO THE HEIGHT OF YOUR FLAT
(How tall do you want your flat?)
SIX-2X2 or 2X4 LUMBER BOARDS CUT TO THE WIDTH OF YOUR FLAT
(How wide do you want your flat?)
HAMMER
NAILS
SAW
HOT GLUE GUN AND GLUE STICKS
AN OLD SHEET
MASKING TAPE
A PENCIL
MARKING PENS or PAINTS and PAINT BRUSHES
PLASTIC MARGARINE TUB FILLED WITH WATER
PAPER TOWELS
OLD LARGE SHIRT

1. Decide how tall and wide your flat will need to be. You must consider where on the set it is going be placed. First you will need to cut your boards to the proper dimensions. You will need four long boards to give your flat the proper height and six shorter boards for the width. This must be duplicated for each flat you need to build.

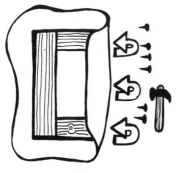

2. Nail two of the long boards to two of the short boards to make a rectangle. Be certain that the edges are flush, meaning the boards are not nailed on top of one another to make the rectangle, but are smooth from one board to the other. You may want to hot glue your boards into position first before nailing together.

3. Lay an old sheet on the ground. Center your wooden frame (the rectangle) in the middle of the sheet. Stretch the sheet so it is tight and smooth across the front. Carefully nail the edges of the sheet to the backside of the wooden frame, pulling the sheet tight so it will be taut (tight) on the front, the side on which you will be painting. You may want to use a hot glue gun before nailing to secure (adhere) the edges of the sheet to the frame.

4. Turn over your flat and dust off any dirt. Using a pencil, sketch (draw) your design on the flat.

5. When you are satisfied with your design, you can either use a permanent marking pen to make outlines or paint in the design, just as you would when creating a backdrop.

6. Let the flat dry completely.

7. Touch-up (re-paint) any areas that need it. Let it dry again.

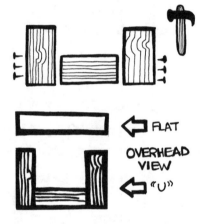

8. You may decide you want your flat to be free-standing. That would mean your flat would lean up against a wall, or something sturdy, so it would not slip or be knocked over during the performance. Preferably, you will build a support system. This is done with three of your remaining short pieces of wood. To begin creating a support for your flat, nail these boards into a "U" shape making the wood pieces flush.

FLAT

OVERHEAD VIEW

"U"

9. Once your "U" is complete, nail it to the bottom short board of your flat. Double-check that you are attaching the "U" to the bottom of your flat and not the top. When you have finished, the four boards (your three from the "U" and the bottom board of the flat) will look like a square. Place the flat over on its side.

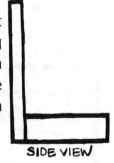

SIDE VIEW

SPECIAL TIP: When attaching your long support boards, put them on sideways instead of flat to offer greater support.

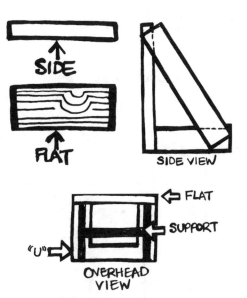

SIDE

FLAT

SIDE VIEW

FLAT

SUPPORT

"U"

OVERHEAD
VIEW

10. Measure the distance between the top of your long boards on the flat and the bottom outer corners of the "U." Mark your remaining long boards to match these measurements. In order for the supporting long boards to be flush against the flat and "U," a small triangle will have to be cut off both ends of the supporting boards so they will be smooth against the flat when nailed. Double-check your measurements before cutting.

FLAT

SUPPORTS

"U"

BACK VIEW

SIDE VIEW

11. Nail a supporting board to each side. When attached properly, these boards will allow your flat to stand by itself. For additional support, you can nail the last short board between the long supporting boards at the halfway point.

12. If you do not have anywhere to store your flat until your performance, you may want to wait to add the supporting pieces until you have your stage area available or on the day of your show.

13. Always make certain that everything is cleaned up and put away after you have finished. Following your show, you can breakdown (take apart) your flat and store (put away) the pieces to be used for future productions!

How to Make Other Kinds of Set Fixtures

These are all done with cardboard, masking tape, paint, scissors and any of your collected supplies.

How to make... a grandfather clock

1. Tape together large pieces of cardboard so they will be the right height to create your Grandfather Clock. Make certain that you add additional taped reinforcement so your clock will not bend.

2. Draw your outline for the clock. Trim any additional cardboard that is not necessary for your design. Paint your clock.

3. Cut a large triangle that is one-third or greater the height of your clock. Fold one of the long edges.

4. Using tape or hot glue, attach the folded part of the triangle to the bottom of the clock. This creates a self-supporting stand.

Trees, Bushes and Flowers

1. Find or tape together a piece of cardboard the correct size to create your desired set piece.

2. Draw your design.

3. Outline and paint.

4. If you choose, cut out your design.

5. Cut a large triangle that is one-third or greater the height of your design. Fold one of the long edges.

6. Using tape or hot glue, attach the folded part of the triangle to the bottom of the design. This creates a self-supporting stand.

Fancy Chairs And Sofas

1. Tape together large pieces of cardboard so they will be the right height and length to create your sofa or chair. Make certain that you add additional taped reinforcement so your pieces will not bend.

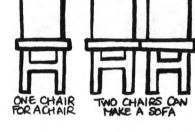

ONE CHAIR FOR A CHAIR   TWO CHAIRS CAN MAKE A SOFA

2. Draw the outline of the sofa or chair back, then paint it.

3. Trim any additional cardboard that is not necessary for your design.

4. Tape your sofa or chair back to the chair(s) you will be using.

5. If there are arms on the chairs you are using to attach the sofa or chair back to, cut slits that will allow the backing to easily slide over them.

Little Things Really Count

The difference between a set and a **PROP** is that a set remains in one position (static) for an entire scene or act, but a prop is picked up, moved from position to position, carried around, and brought on and/or taken off stage during a performance. Simply put, a prop is something that is portable.

The word prop is actually short for **PROPERTIES**. They are called properties because the items could be the belongings of the characters, the office or region in which the show takes place.

Most props can be borrowed such as books, playing cards, plastic dishes and plastic cups. However it can be more fun, and easier, to make your own sometimes. You can really let your imagination go wild when you are making props!

How to Make Some of Your Own Props

Here are a few ideas to help you get started.

Listed below are some supplies you may want to gather to make your props. These same items will be used to make the puppets on pages 41 and 77-83. Always remember to ask permission before borrowing anything and remember to clean up when you are finished.

CARDBOARD	CLEAR PACKAGE TAPE
WHITE GLUE	CONSTRUCTION PAPER
MASKING TAPE	HOLE PUNCHER
PENCILS	SCISSORS
PERMANENT MARKING PENS	NON-TOXIC POSTER PAINT
PAINT BRUSHES	TISSUE PAPER
WRAPPING PAPER	OLD SHEETS
NEWSPAPER	PLASTIC CONTAINER LIDS
PAPER PLATES	PLASTIC MARGARINE TUB
OLD LARGE SHIRT	PAPER TOWELS
GLITTER	POPSICLE STICKS
COTTON	PLASTIC OR STYROFOAM CUPS
TOILET PAPER ROLLS	PAPER TOWEL ROLLS
BRADS	PIPECLEANERS
PAPERCLIPS	TINFOIL
PAPER MUFFIN CUPS	EGG CARTONS

IDEA: You may want to start your own collection of supplies for future projects. A large box is a great place to store things and it will make items easier to find!

Props You Can Make

Flowers in Pots

1. Draw your flower shape onto a piece of construction paper or cardboard. Cut it out.

2. Place a drop of white, craft or hot glue in the center of your flower and attach a popsicle stick or pipecleaner to act as the stem.

3. Cut out two circles to become the center for your flower. Glue one to each side, making certain you cover the end of the pipecleaner or popsicle stick stem.

4. Find a container, such as a margarine tub or small box, and decorate it to make the pot.

5. Crumple up some newspaper or tissue paper and place it into the bottom of the pot. Make certain that the paper is in the pot firmly so the flower can stand up. You may want to glue it down. Another possibility is to use a piece of styrofoam in the bottom.

6. Place your flower(s) into the pot, arranging as desired.

7. If you would like to add leaves, cut out leaf shapes and attach them to the stems before placing into the flowerpot.

Telephone

1. Gather together a small box, a toilet paper roll, two paper or styrofoam cups, black paint, white paper and a piece of string.

2. Use masking tape to attach the cups securely to each end of the toilet paper roll.

3. Paint the toilet paper roll, cups, string and box all black (or desired color).

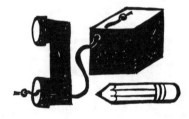

4. Use a sharp pencil or the point of a pair of scissors to poke a small hole into the bottom of one of the cups and a corner of the box. Thread the string through the holes and knot at each end (inside the cup and inside the box).

5. Cut a circle out of white paper and add numbers around the outside to create a dial. If you prefer, you can create a push-button style phone by cutting a square out of white paper and adding the numbers in sequence.

6. Glue dial to the box.

Candlestick

You can make your candlesticks a variety of heights and sizes.

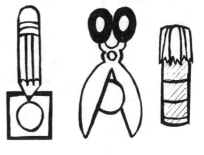

1. Trace the end of a cardboard tube onto a piece of heavy paper. Cut it out and tape it securely to the end of the tube.

2. Select a small box, jar lid or something with an interesting shape, but flat bottom and top, and attach to the open end of the cardboard tube so it will stand.

3. Paint and let dry.

4. Cut out a flame shape, adding a small tail to the bottom. Cut two more flame shapes slightly smaller than the first, from a different color. Glue one to each side of first flame. Cut two additional flames that are still smaller and of a third color and glue onto flame.

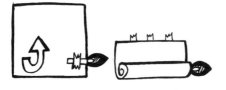

5. Tape the flame to the edge of a piece of construction paper and roll tightly into a tube. Tape the edge securely.

6. Glue or tape the candle to the top of the candlestick.

Picture Frame

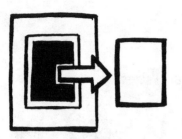

1. Find a piece of cardboard and cut it to the size of the frame you want. Trace around your selected picture to determine the size of the picture opening.

2. Cut one inch inside of the tracing to create the frame opening.

3. Paint and decorate.

4. Tape your picture onto the back of the frame, face down.

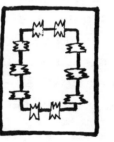

5. To make a stand, cut a cardboard triangle, at least one-third the size of the frame, and fold over one of the long sides.

Picture Perfect

6. Glue or tape to the back of the frame.

Clock

1. Find a box the size you would like for your clock.

2. Paint the outside of the box.

3. Cut a small circle out of some construction paper. This will be your dial. Also cut out two small arrows, one shorter than the other. These will be the hands of your clock.

4. Write numbers on the clock face.

5. Glue face onto one side of the box.

6. Use the point of a pair of scissors, punch a small hole into the center of the clock face and through the box. Then, use the scissors or hole punch to put a hole in the bottom of each arrow.

7. Use a brad to attach the hands through the clock face and the box. Set your time. If you prefer, you may also paint the clock hands directly onto the face of the clock.

Plate of Spaghetti

1. Get a paper plate, yellow or white yarn, and white glue.

2. Cover the middle of the plate with glue.

3. Arrange the yarn into spaghetti, adding more glue as you continue.

4. Cut brown construction paper or use brown pom poms to make meatballs. Glue them to the spaghetti.

5. Put some thick red paint on the top of the spaghetti to add sauce.

Magic Wand

1. Cut two stars of the same size out of construction paper or cardboard.

2. Decorate one side of each star using glitter, sequins, paint, etc.

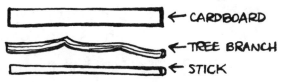

3. Select a long stick, such as a dowel rod or tree branch, or cut a piece of cardboard for the wand.

4. Cut some ribbon or long pieces of tissue paper to make streamers.

5. Sandwich the stick and streamers between the undecorated sides of the stars and glue together.

Telescope/Spyglass

1. Gather two cardboard paper towel rolls and one cardboard toilet paper roll.

2. Cut through the side of one of the paper towel rolls. Out of the other paper towel roll, cut a small strip of about 1/4-inch in width.

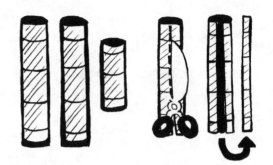

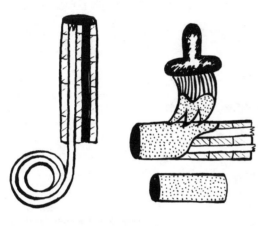

3. Tape the strip into the cut of the first paper towel roll. This will slightly increase the width of the roll.

4. Paint both the enlarged paper towel roll and the toilet paper roll a desired color or cover with construction paper.

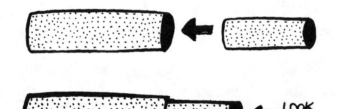

LOOK
THROUGH
HERE

5. Slide the smaller roll into the larger roll. It should fit fairly securely. To add additional authenticity, you may add a small strip of foil to each end of your telescope.

Wagon

1. Find a box that will be large enough to be the body of your wagon.

2. Paint the box.

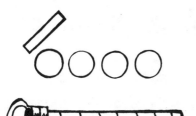

3. Cut four same-sized circles for the wheels. Also cut one strip about three inches wide and eight inches long out of cardboard.

4. Securely tape the cardboard strip to the end of a cardboard wrapping paper roll or two towel rolls taped together to make the handle.

5. Paint the wheels and the handle.

6. Measure and mark where you would like to place the wheels. Place a hole at each of your four marks and then into the center of each wheel. Attach the wheels to the wagon with brads.

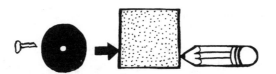

7. Cut four matching slits at the bottom end of the handle. Press the sections back to look like a flower. Put a hole in the center of each section. Put the handle in position at the front end of the wagon. Mark, then make the matching holes in the wagon body. Attach the handle with brads.

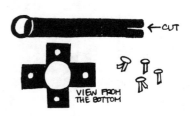

What other props can you create? Look around your house, school, virtually anywhere, for ideas.

On Fingers, On Hands, On Strings... Everywhere!

PUPPETS are an extremely old form of storytelling and theatre. In many countries, they are still used to tell the same fables and legends that have been told and been handed down for generations.

In Thailand and Malaysia, **SHADOW PUPPETS** tell the stories. The puppeteers perform behind a thin cloth, sometimes called a scrim, that is lit from behind. You can create the same kind of theatre by hanging up a sheet and shining a light on it from behind.

HAND PUPPETS are very popular in England, especially the characters Punch and Judy, whose original purpose was to satirize (make fun of) certain political figures and ideas. **MARIONETTES**, puppets controlled overhead by strings, are favorites in Italy and France.

Working with puppets can be a great way to become familiar with and start creating your own shows. It will give you the opportunity to invent stories, characters and character voices, design small sets and props, and test your imagination.

WHAT IS A PUPPET?

How to Make Puppets

You have already seen how to make a Shadow Puppet in the chapter on CREATING YOUR OWN TECHNICAL EFFECTS. Here are some other types of puppets you can make.

Tube Finger Puppet

1. With the base of your finger at the edge of a piece of construction paper, mark just past the tip of your finger.

2. Wrap enough of the paper around your finger to make a tube. Trim the paper at the mark you made in step 1. Secure the tube with some tape.

3. Decorate the tube (using buttons, markers, yarn, etc.) to create your puppet.

Felt Finger Puppet

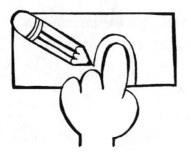

1. Trace around your finger on a piece of felt adding 1/4 inch extra.

2. Cut out two of the traced shapes. Glue or sew the edges carefully together. If you glue, make certain you allow plenty of drying time.

3. Decorate using buttons, markers, yarn, etc.

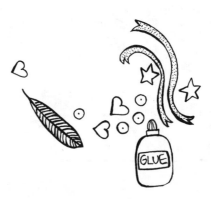

Glove Finger Puppets

1. Find an old glove that you can use. Knit gloves, rubber kitchen gloves, gardening gloves, even formal gloves will all work. Each will give you a different texture and look for your puppets.

RUBBER KITCHEN GLOVES

FORMAL GLOVES

KNIT SNOW GLOVES

GARDENING GLOVES

2. Decorate using buttons, markers, yarn, etc.

With glove puppets, you can create an entire story with one hand — or make a whole puppet family!

Painted Puppet

To create a painted puppet, you will need to use special makeup paints (see the chapter on WHY DO WE NEED MAKEUP?, page 109). There are two different types of painted puppets you can make. One is painted directly onto the fingers and the other directly onto the side of the hand.

Finger Puppets

1. Gather special makeup paints.

2. Paint your finger tips with the palm facing toward you. Give each a different character.

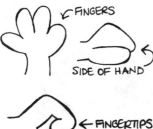

Side of Hand Puppet

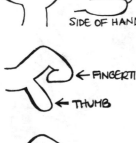

1. Gather special makeup paints

2. Curl you fingers into the palm and close the thumb over the tips.

3. Paint the eyes of your puppet on the top part of the hand, creating the top half of the face. Then add the top lip just where the thumb meets the curled hand. The lower lip should be painted on the thumb.

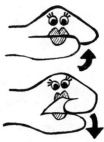

4. Move your thumb up and down to make the puppet talk. Add hair, eyelashes, a mustache or anything you want to finish your puppet.

Sock Puppet

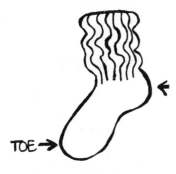

1. Find an old, used, clean sock.

2. Put the sock over your hand so the sock heel is on your wrist and your fingers are in the toes.

3. Tuck the toe of the sock between your fingers and thumb to make a mouth.

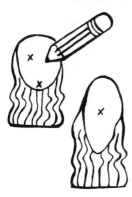

4. Close your fingers and thumb together. Mark where you want to place the eyes and nose. If you want to include a tongue, add a mark inside the mouth where you would like to place a tongue.

5. Take the sock off your hand. Attach the eyes, nose and tongue. Decorate using buttons, markers, yarn, etc.

Toe Dancer Puppet

1. Use a piece of cardboard or heavy piece of paper and draw your puppet shape.

2. Use a nickel or the cap of a bottle to trace two circles toward the bottom of your shape.

3. Cut out the shape and the two circles.

4. Decorate using buttons, markers, yarn, etc.

5. Stick your fingers through the holes to appear as the legs to your puppet.

Marionette

1. Trace onto and cut out of heavy paper or cardboard one body, two upper arms, two lower arms with hands, two upper legs and two lower legs with feet.

2. Place holes in all the pieces where indicated in illustration.

3. Decorate, being careful not to cover up any of the holes.

4. Connect the pieces of the puppet together, as shown, using brads.

5. Thread ribbon, yarn or string through the remaining holes in the head, hands and feet. Tie them to one or two sticks.

Puppets are used around the world, from China to Italy to Brazil, to tell famous stories. What kinds of stories can you tell using your puppets?

Collecting and Making

COSTUMES are the clothes that actors wear during a show. Sometimes costumes resemble clothing we wear everyday. Others represent specific time periods and still others are really fancy and crazy, like something from outer space.

Costumes can be fun to create because you can use old clothes, recyclables, various ideas and mix them together in different ways. All of the parts that make up a costume are called COSTUME PIECES. Skirts, shirts and pants are all considered costume pieces.

ACCESSORIES are all the little things that can be added to a costume. Eyeglasses, purses, shoes, socks and jewelry are all accessories.

You may want to start your own COSTUME WARDROBE, a collection of all sorts of costumes and accessories, for shows. Halloween costumes are a great way to begin your collection. Some of your old clothing, or even things from friends and family, also make great additions. You may want to get a large box so you can store everything in one convenient place.

All About Costumes

Clothing comes in many styles because fashion is constantly changing. Fancy. Formal. Everyday. Summer. Winter. There is special clothing for astronauts, cowboys, doctors and athletes. There are long and short clothes, dark and light colored clothes, even clothing that people wear to celebrate their culture. Here is a list of some of the things you may want to collect for your wardrobe.

COSTUME PIECES

SHIRTS/T-SHIRTS · DRESSES · SKIRTS · COATS/SWEATERS

VESTS · SWEATSHIRTS/SWEATPANTS · PANTS/SHORTS/LEGGINGS

PETTICOATS · LEOTARDS/TIGHTS · CAPES/SHAWLS

OLD SHEETS · HALLOWEEN COSTUMES

ACCESSORIES

EYEGLASSES · NECKLACES · RINGS · BELTS

SCARVES · NECKTIES · SHOES · SOCKS · GLOVES · EARRINGS · HATS

SUSPENDERS · FEATHER BOA · KNEEPADS · SWEATBANDS

WATCHES · BRACELETS · BROOCHES (PINS)

Can you think of any other costume pieces or accessories you might be able to add to your collection?

How to Make Some of Your Own Costumes and Accessories

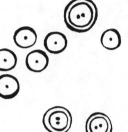

Supplies for costume, accessory and puppet decoration and creation

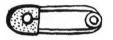

NEWSPAPER · WHITE GLUE · SAFETY PINS · GLITTER · MASKING TAPE

STRING · FEATHERS · BEADS · RIBBON · PERMANENT MARKING PENS

NON-TOXIC PAINT · PAINT BRUSHES · CARDBOARD · YARN

CONSTRUCTION PAPER · PIPECLEANERS · ALUMINUM FOIL

ALUMINUM PIE PLATES · SCISSORS · HOLE PUNCHER · PENCIL · STICKERS

PLASTIC DRINKING STRAWS · TISSUE PAPER · WRAPPING PAPER

CELLOPHANE · BRADS · OLD SOCKS · HEADBANDS

FAKE FUR · FELT · COTTON BALLS · SEQUINS · EGG CARTONS

TINSEL · BUTTONS · SEWING NEEDLE & THREAD · ELASTIC

HOT GLUE GUN & GLUE

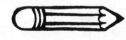

Once you get started finding things to add to your costumes, you will be surprised at how many different kinds of costumes and accessories you can make!

Fun Costumes and Accessories You Can Make

Cardboard Cutout
For all your shirts, you will need to follow these first two instructions:

1. Lay your t-shirt on a piece of heavy cardboard and trace around it adding a two-inch allowance. Cut out the pattern.

2. Pull your t-shirt over the cardboard cutout. This will stretch the fabric and make it easier to decorate.

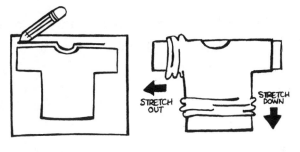

Formal Shirt
(see above for cardboard cutout)

1. Cut six pieces of ribbon twice as long as the length of the t-shirt.

2. Measure out a piece of thread a little bit longer than the length of the t-shirt. Thread a needle and knot one end.

3. Sew long stiches down the length of the ribbon. When you reach the end, gather the ribbon. Tie a knot after gathering material. Repeat with the other five ribbons.

4. Begin at the center of the t-shirt and work outward. Attach the ribbons to the front of the t-shirt either by sewing or with hot glue. Add a black bow at the neck to complete the look.

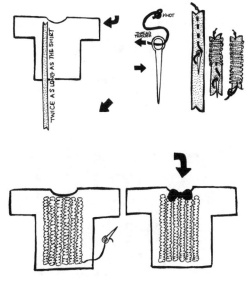

Shirt With Vest

(see page 87 for cardboard cutout)

1. Use a pencil to draw your vest design on your t-shirt. Add a tie.

2. Use a dark, permanent marker for pinstripes and pockets.

3. Paint the vest.

4. Add buttons and a piece of gold braid for the finishing touch.

Baseball T-Shirt
(see page 87 for cardboard cutout)

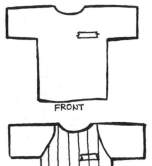

1. Place a small piece of tape on the front of the t-shirt where you want the team name to go.

2. Draw lines lightly with a pencil. Use a dark, permanent marker for stripes, leaving shoulder area plain.

3. Remove the masking tape and write in the team name with permanent marker.

4. Use masking tape on the back of the t-shirt to block off a large area for the player's number and name. Then follow instruction in step #2 for striping.

5. Remove masking tape and add the player's name and number in permanent marker.

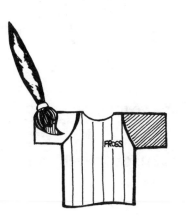

6. Paint the sleeves in a contrasting color if desired.

Fancy Skirt

1. Turn an old, clean sheet sideways. Paint and decorate.

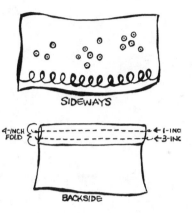

2. Turn the sheet over so the decoration is face down. Fold the top edge of the sheet down about four inches. Sew a single seam from side to side about one inch below the fold. Sew a second seam about three inches below the fold.

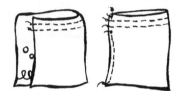

3. Turn the sheet back over so the decorated side is face up. Fold the sheet in half so the decorated side is turned in on itself and the short edges are touching. Sew together the short edges, but leave the section between the two seams open.

4. Measure a piece of elastic around the waist of the performer. Make certain the elastic is not stretched too tightly. Cut it about one inch longer than needed to circle the waist comfortably. Put a safety pin in each end of the elastic.

5. Safety pin one end of the elastic to the fold of the fabric, and push the other safety pin through between the seams until it comes out the other end.

6. Tie the ends of the elastic together. Remove the safety pins. Turn the skirt inside out.

7. Trim the bottom with scissors, use masking tape or stitch with thread to make a hem if the skirt is too long.

Mummy

1. Take an old, clean sheet and cut it into strips about three inches in width.

2. Sew the strips together end to end, making about six long strips.

3. Roll up your strips to make them easier to handle.

4. Wrap up your mummy (actor) using one strip each for the arms, legs, body and head, carefully pinning into place.

TO MAKE YOUR MUMMY LOOK OLD TRY THIS: Make some tea in a large pot and dip the strips into it. Lay them out in the sun and let them dry completely. Don't worry if the color is not even, that makes it look even more realistic. To make it even scarier, check out the **Mummy Makeup** in the next chapter.

Magician's Robe

1. Take an old, clean sheet and turn it sideways. Decorate.

2. Turn the sheet over so the decorated side is face down, then fold in each short side so they meet in the center of the sheet.

3. Measure down from the top of the sheet along the fold about twelve inches and mark. From the twelve inch mark, measure twenty-four inches toward the center and mark. Repeat on the other side.

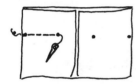

4. Sew from the twelve inch mark on the outside directly across in a straight seam to the twenty-four inch mark, making certain you are sewing the front to the back. Repeat on the other side.

5. Cut along the fold from the top edge of the sheet to the seam. Repeat on the other side creating arm holes.

6. Measure from the cut corner of the sheet across the top toward center twenty-four inches. Mark. Sew top of sheet closed from the corner to the mark. Repeat with other side.

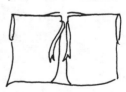

7. Add ribbon to the neck to close robe.

ANOTHER VERSION: Follow the directions #1 and #2 for making the Fancy Skirt (pg. 90) Skip #3 and go to #4 **EXCEPT** use ribbon or cord and measure the length around the neck area and then double it. Follow direction #5 and, when done, tie a knot in each end of the ribbon or cord.

SIDEWAYS

Newspaper Hat #1

1. Take a piece of newspaper and turn it sideways so the fold is across the top.

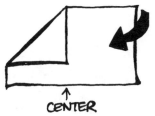

CENTER

2. Fold one of the top corners down toward the center of the paper, making a triangle. Repeat with the other corner.

3. Fold up the bottom edge of one side of the newspaper so it overlaps the triangles.

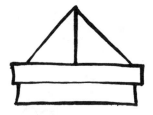

4. Turn the paper over and repeat #3.

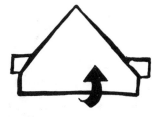 

5. Decorate using buttons, markers, yarn, etc.

Newspaper Hat # 2

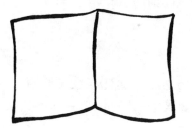

1. Open up a sheet of newspaper.

2. Place it on your head and smash it down around the crown.

3. Have someone use masking tape to make a loose band at about eyebrow level.

4. Roll the extra paper up to create a brim or cut off in a design.

5. Decorate using buttons, markers, yarn, ect.

Space Helmet

1. Find a box large enough to fit comfortably over your head.

2. Have someone mark half circles on the side of the box where your shoulders sit.

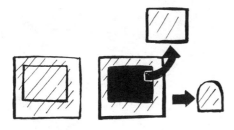

3. Remove the box and mark where you would like the opening of the helmet.

4. Cut out both half circles and the front of the helmet.

5. Find two matching jar lids and two pipecleaners. Twist the pipecleaners into a crazy antenna.

6. Cover the box, two lids, and pipecleaner antennae in tinfoil.

7. Glue the lids to the side of the box in the ear area. Poke a hole in the top of the box and insert the antenna, securing it with tape inside.

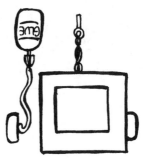

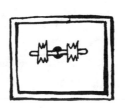

Princess Hat With Braids

You can also use this design as a magician's or a halloween witch's hat!

1. Take several sheets of newspaper and open them up into a stack.

2. Using one corner of the newspapers to become the point; roll the newspapers into a cone.

3. Press the cone flat and masking tape the edge securely so the newspapers will not unroll. Trim off the bottom of the cone to give it a straight, even edge.

4. Decorate using buttons, markers, yarn, etc.

5. Decide the length of the braids you would like and double that length in yarn. Cut about ten matching lengths of yarn and one small piece to tie tightly about the center of the yarn. Put together another bundle to make the second braid.

6. Use your tie at the center as the top of the braid. Divide yarn into three equal sections to braid.

LEFT OVER MIDDLE   RIGHT OVER MIDDLE   LEFT OVER MIDDLE   RIGHT OVER MIDDLE

7. Braid by taking the left section over the middle section, then the right section over the new middle section, then repeating all the way to the bottom. Secure end of braid with rubber band, yarn or piece of ribbon.

8. Attach braids securely to the left and right insides of the hat.

Bracelets

1. Gather together a variety of cardboard tubes.

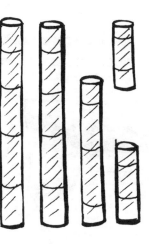

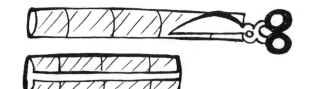

2. Turn them on their sides and cut a slit from one end to the other.

3. Cut the tubes into different widths.

4. Decorate using buttons, markers, yarn, etc.

5. Wrap around wrists.

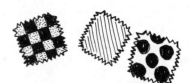

Shoe Covers

Shoe covers can be made out of just about any kind of fabric—felt, leftover pieces of material, even old sheets work great.

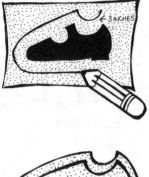

1. Fold a piece of fabric in half with the right (designed) sides together. Use the shoe you want to cover as a pattern by turning it on its side on the fabric and tracing three inches around it.

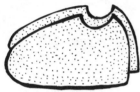

2. Cut out two covers. Use your cutout as a pattern and cut two more for the second shoe cover.

3. Sew or hot glue two pieces of fabric together from toe to top opening of shoe and from heel to the top opening of shoe, leaving the bottom and top open. Repeat with second cover.

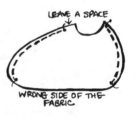

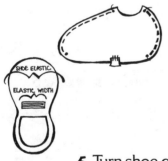

4. Attach, by sewing or hot gluing, a piece of elastic (a little shorter than the width of the shoe that will be covered) to the middle of each side of the bottom of the shoe cover. Repeat with other shoe cover.

5. Turn shoe covers inside out and decorate.

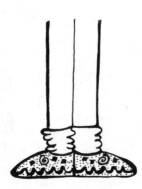

Animal Tails

1. Gather together three different colors of yarn, ribbon cord or fabric and cut them to even lengths.

2. Knot together one end and then follow step #7 of **Princess hat with braids** (pg. 96) to make tail braid.

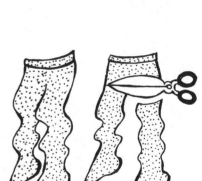

3. Make a small loop at the top of the braid and secure by sewing or using a safety pin.

4. Thread yarn, ribbon or cord through the loop. Knot each end and tie around waist.

Or Version Two

1. Find an old pair of clean, colorful tights or a knee-high sock.

2. Cut off one leg if using tights.

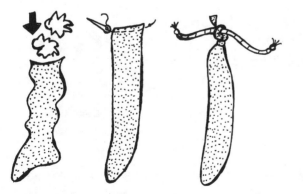

3. Stuff the leg with crumpled newspaper, paper towels, cotton or scraps of fabric until firm, but not too hard or stiff.

4. Sew or hot glue the top opening closed.

5. Tie the end of the tight in a knot around a piece of yarn, cord or ribbon. Knot each end, and tie around waist.

Animal Ears

1. Draw the shape of the ear you want on a piece of construction paper. Remember that you will need to cut this shape larger than the actual size of the ear you are making.

2. Cut out two of the shapes.

3. Cut out two smaller sizes of the same shape in contrasting colors for the inner ears.

4. Glue the smaller shapes into the bottom center of each of the larger shapes.

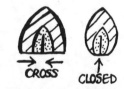

5. Make a small cut up from the bottom center, almost to the middle of the inner ear shapes.

6. Pull one side of the bottom of each ear over the other side. Securely tape or glue closed in that position.

7. Make two small cuts in the bottom of each ear. Push the outside pieces back and the middle piece forward.

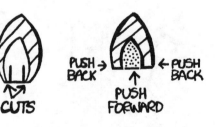

8. Tape or glue the pushed out pieces of the ears onto a headband or if you prefer, pin them directly in the hair.

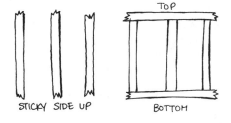

Yarn Wig

1. Lay out three pieces of masking tape, about six inches long each, sticky side facing up.

2. Cut two more six-inch pieces of masking tape and lay one piece, sticky side up, across the top of the three original strips of tape and one across the bottom.

3. Cut enough six-inch yarn pieces to be carefully placed along and to fill the edge of the bottom piece of tape. This will be the front of your wig.

4. Cut enough twelve-inch yarn pieces to be carefully placed along and to fill the edge of the top tape. This will be the back of your wig.

5. Cut enough thirty-inch yarn pieces to be carefully placed along and fill the three strips of tape. This will be the sides of your wig.

6. Try on the wig and have someone trim it evenly for the length you need. Make sure you get your own hair out of the way before cutting!

Wig Cap: You can make your own wig cap by cutting off the toe of an old (but clean) used stocking or nylon. If your hair is long, you should pin it up, then pull the wig cap over your hair on top of your head. If your hair is short, pull the wig cap on and then tuck your hair up underneath it. Secure the edges of the wig cap to your hair with bobby pins or wig pins to keep it from slipping off!

Eyeglasses
You can make really wild and crazy designs.

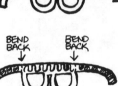

1. Find a small piece of cardboard, about twice the width of your face. Mark the cardboard into thirds.

2. In the center of the cardboard, between your middle marks, draw you eyeglass design.

3. Add your earpieces.

4. Cut out the eyeglasses including the eyeholes.

5. Decorate.

6. Fold back the earpieces.

7. **To Make Sunglasses:** Cut small pieces of colored cellophane and attach the back of the eyeglasses over the eyeholes.

Another Idea!

1. Get four pipecleaners.

2. Twist two of them into circles, leaving a small tail.

3. Twist together the two tails to create a nose bridge for the glasses.

4. Use the remaining two pipecleaners to make the earpieces.

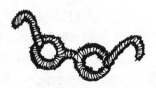

Purse
Try using some different shaped boxes for your purse designs!

1. Find a small, empty cereal box and tape the opened end closed.

2. Turn the box on its side and mark a point that is about one-third the way down the side of the box. Cut the box all the way through at this point.

3. Tape the box together again, but only across at the back seam.

4. Decorate.

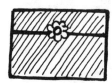

5. Glue something interesting on the front side of the box at the center of the upper part. It should appear to be the purse clasp.

6. Poke one hole in each side of the lower part of the purse, just below the cut if you would like to make a hand or shoulder bag. Thread a piece of ribbon, cord or yarn through the holes from the inside of the purse. Knot on the inside.

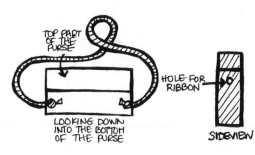

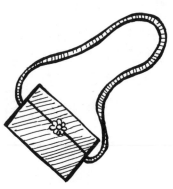

Paper Bag Mask

1. Find a paper bag large enough to go over your head.

2. Slip one hand inside the paperbag and place it right in front of your eyes. With the hand on the outside of the bag, mark where your eyes are. Be very careful while doing this.

3. Have someone mark where your shoulders are and cut out the shoulders and eyeholes just as in steps #2 & #3 for the **Space Helmet** (pg. 95).

4. Use your creativity and decorate.

Version Two

1. Follow the above steps #1 & #2.

2. Mark where your nose is.

3. Take off the bag and draw a silly nose.

4. Cut out the eyes and trim off the area just below the silly nose area.

5. Decorate.

Mardi Gras Mask

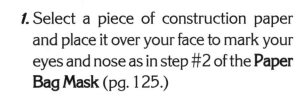

1. Select a piece of construction paper and place it over your face to mark your eyes and nose as in step #2 of the **Paper Bag Mask** (pg. 125.)

2. Cut out the eyeholes.

3. Draw the shape for your mask design and cut it out.

4. Decorate.

5. Attach a stick to your mask or you can poke a small hole in each side of the mask and thread through a ribbon or elastic.

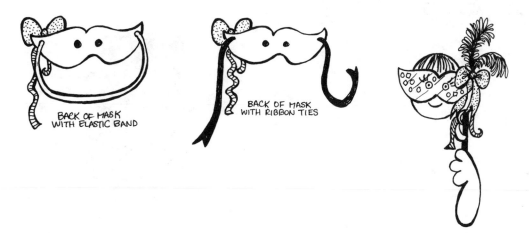

BACK OF MASK WITH ELASTIC BAND

BACK OF MASK WITH RIBBON TIES

Magician's Beard

1. Select a piece of cardboard or heavy construction paper and draw your beard shape.

2. Cut out the beard.

3. Poke a small hole in each of the upper corners of the beard and twist a pipecleaner through each one.

4. Cover the cut-out with glue and use cotton balls or yarn to make hair of beard.

5. Hook pipecleaners over ears after the glue is dry.

Cardboard Mustaches

There are all different styles and combinations you can create
with beards and mustaches.

1. Find a small piece of cardboard or heavy piece of
construction paper and draw your mustache.

2. Place your thumb at the center of the top of your
design and draw around it, creating a "U" shape.

"U"-SHAPE

3. Cut out the mustache and the "U."

4. Decorate.

5. Stick the "U" into your nose to wear the mustache. It will tickle a little.

"U" GOES INTO THE NOSE

These items will give you a good start for your wardrobe. Keep your eyes
open for all sorts of things that you can use for costumes and accessories in
your shows!

Faces for Your Show and for Fun

Most performances in theatre require that everybody wear some **MAKEUP**. This is because the special lighting that is used in shows is extremely bright and would wash out everybody's natural face coloring on the stage. In other words, without any makeup, the audience would have great difficulty seeing the faces of the actors during the performance.

The first part of the makeup that is applied (put on) is called **BASE**. Base makes the face all one color so the other colors applied will appear brighter and more defined. After the base, **POWDER** is put on. The powder sets the makeup so that under the hot lights, the makeup will not melt off.

Once you have completed your base and powder you can add whatever colors and designs are required for your production. Bushy eyebrows, glamorous eyelashes, rosy cheeks and scary scars help to bring your characters to life. You can become a clown or, just as easily, a villain. With makeup, you can even be a cat!

WHY DO WE NEED MAKEUP?

Makeup Fun

Makeup is really fun, but it can also be very messy. Always make sure that you wear an old, big shirt that you can get makeup on. Halloween is a great time of the year to find makeup kits that contain many colors.

Different kinds of makeup

There are two basic types of makeup that are used on stage.

WATER

SPONGE

WATER-BASED makeup comes in both a liquid or cake form. If you use a cake, you will put a little water on a makeup sponge and rub it over the cake to pick up the color. Then you gently apply it to your skin using the sponge in even strokes.

WATER-BASE CAKE

GREASEPAINT POT

GREASEPAINT does not need to have any water added to it and it goes on to the skin very smoothly. But, you need to make certain to powder really well because greasepaint can smear very easily. Greasepaint comes in makeup sticks and makeup pots. Both types can be applied with sponges or makeup brushes, which work particularly well if you are doing intricate designs.

GREASEPAINT TUBE

THIN LINER BRUSH

It is very important that you ALWAYS test out any makeup you are planning on using to make certain you do not have allergies to a certain kind. First, put a little on a small area and leave it on for a little bit to see how your skin reacts. If there is no reaction, say a reddening of the skin, bumps or a rash, then there should be no problem. However, if it is red or bumpy, you may need to find a different kind of makeup to use.

Makeup comes in many different shapes, forms and colors.

BASE MAKEUP is usually the same color as your skin, but can be darker or lighter for special characters. Base makeup can be water-based or greasepaint and is applied evenly with a sponge over the face and neck.

EYESHADOWS are the bright colors that are most often used on the eyelid, although for some specialty makeups, such as animals, they can be used anywhere on the face. Eyeshadows come in a small dry cake to which you do not have to add water or a loose powder. It looks a little bit like glitter. Eyeshadow can be applied with a makeup brush or a cotton swab.

LIPSTICK comes in a tube or a paint pot and can be applied directly from the tube with a finger or with a makeup brush.

LIPLINER comes in both pencil or liquid pen form and is used for outlining lips and can be applied directly to the lips.

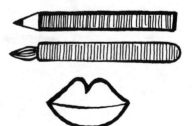

EYELINER and **EYEBROW PENCILS** are both used for outlining eyes and darkening eyebrows. These also come as makeup pencils or liquid pens and can be applied directly.

MASCARA is used to darken and lengthen the eyelashes. It can also be used to color or highlight beards and mustaches.

BLUSHER, or **BLUSH,** is a colored powder applied to the cheek area with a large, soft makeup brush. Lipstick can also provide a blush color when gently applied with the fingertips to the cheekbone area.

POWDER can be either white or tinted (lightly colored) and is applied with a powder puff, then gently dusted off with a large, soft makeup brush. This is how the makeup is set.

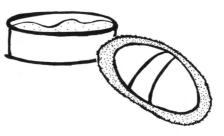

MAKEUP KITS can be found at costume shops and around Halloween at a variety of locations. Each makeup kit will have several different colors and comes in both greasepaint or water-based sets.

How to Do Your Own Makeup

Doing your own makeup takes lots of practice and many people rehearse putting on their makeup the same way they practice running lines for a show.

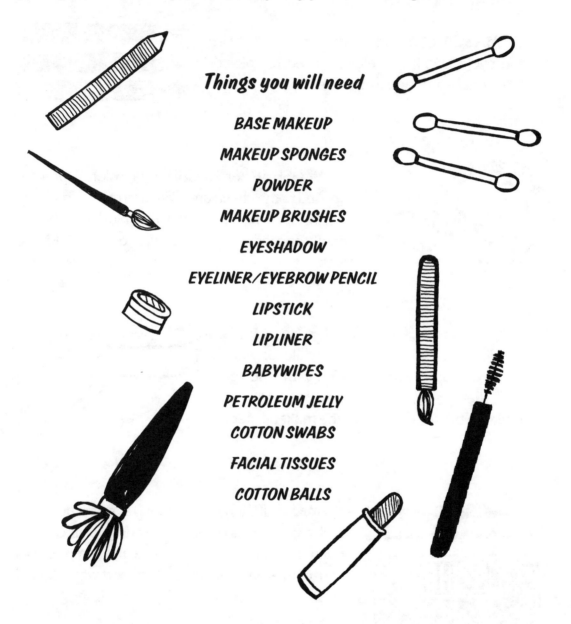

Things you will need

BASE MAKEUP

MAKEUP SPONGES

POWDER

MAKEUP BRUSHES

EYESHADOW

EYELINER/EYEBROW PENCIL

LIPSTICK

LIPLINER

BABYWIPES

PETROLEUM JELLY

COTTON SWABS

FACIAL TISSUES

COTTON BALLS

A shoebox or fishing tackle box is a great way to store your makeup.

Basic Makeup

Here are some makeup instructions to help you get started. Basic makeup is the foundation for all the other makeup you will create.

1. Apply the base makeup evenly and smoothly over the entire face with a sponge.

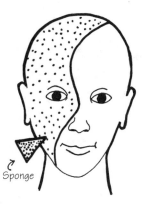

2. Powder.

3. Gently brush off any loose powder with a large, soft makeup brush.

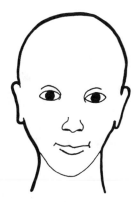

Now you are ready to begin your full makeup application!

TIP: If you make a mistake, dampen the end of a cotton swab and gently wipe away. Then you can correct your mistake.

Glamour Makeup

Follow basic makeup steps #1 through #3 on page 113.

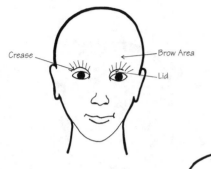

Crease — Brow Area — Lid

1. Apply eyeshadow to the eyelid. Use a darker shade of or different contrasting color for the crease (fold) of the eye. For added effect, use a lighter shade of color in the area between the crease and eyebrow.

2. Draw in eyebrows.

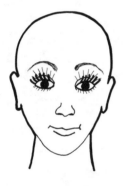

3. Outline eyes with eyeliner and use mascara on eyelashes.

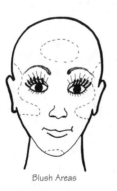

Blush Areas

4. Use blush on cheeks and then lightly on chin, forehead and temples (the sides of the head between the eyes and hairline).

5. Outline the lips with liner. Fill them in with lipstick.

Men's Makeup

Follow basic makeup steps #1 through #3 on page 113.

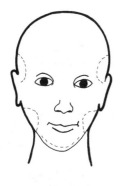

1. Add a dark blush to the temples, jawline and hollows of the cheeks. To find the hollows, suck in your cheeks to find the depressions.

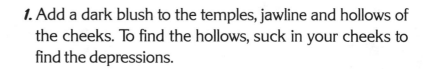

2. Add a little dark pencil to the eyebrows.

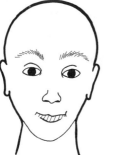

3. Use a shade of lipstick a little darker than natural coloring.

4. Mustache: To make a mustache, use black or dark brown eyeliner and draw your mustache design above the upper lip. Use additional pencils in lighter and contrasting colors to add highlights. Powder.

KITCHEN SPONGE

5. Beard Stubble: Cut a small piece from a clean, unused kitchen sponge (this is important in order to achieve the right effect) and dab in brown or black makeup. Tap very lightly over the lower half of the face.

IDEA: Try on your cardboard mustaches, eyeglasses, beards, wigs and other accessories with some of these makeups!

Bruise

Follow basic makeup steps #1 through #3 on page 113.

1. Take purple greasepaint and rub it with a fingertip across the area that needs to look bruised.

2. Rub some blue greasepaint along one edge and blend into the purple.

3. Rub some yellow greasepaint around part of the other edge and blend into the purple.

4. Add a red greasepaint spot between the blue and purple for added effect. Be sure to experiment with different colors and remember to always blend your colors together for the most realistic effect.

Scar

1. Use either a lipliner pencil or greasepaint that is a shade lighter than your base makeup to draw your scar shape a little wider than you want your scar to appear.

2. Use a pencil or greasepaint with a thin brush in a shade darker than your base makeup to draw the scar shape directly onto the lighter area. Blend dark color very gently into lighter shade. Powder.

3. Use any color greasepaint or lipliner to add stitches for added effect. Powder.

Old Lady / Old Man

Follow basic makeup steps #1 through #3 on page 113.

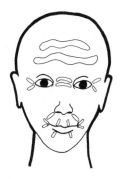

1. Wrinkle up your forehead, eyes, nose and lips. Using a shade lighter than your base makeup, fill in the wrinkles in all those areas and gently blend into base.

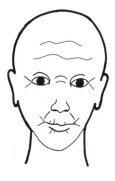

2. Wrinkle again, then use a dark pencil to draw in all the wrinkles. Gently blend the dark lines into the lighter shade.

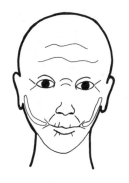

3. Puff out your cheeks and trace around the bottom of the cheek from the mouth to the ear in a lighter shade. Blend.

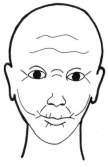

4. Puff out your cheeks again and use a dark pencil over the lighter color. Blend gently.

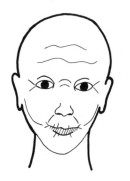

5. Fill in your lips with a natural shade and powder.

Crooked Nose

Follow basic makeup steps #1 through #3 on page 113.

1. Use a shade darker than your base to draw a line down each side of your nose.

2. Blend the makeup down into the base so it stays darker toward the center of the nose, but becomes lighter toward the cheek area. This is creating a **LOWLIGHT**.

3. Using a shade lighter than your base, draw your crooked nose shape down the bridge of your nose. This is called creating a **HIGHLIGHT**.

4. Gently blend the edge of the lighter shade into the darker shade.

Highlight: A highlight in makeup means that you place a lighter shade over a portion of your face to make it brighter and pick up the light. Many people use lighter shades on their cheek bones (just under the eyes), down the bridge of their nose (the center), on their chin and on their forehead to create certain illusions on their faces.

Lowlight: A lowlight does just the opposite of a highlight by making a certain area on the face appear darker. Many people use lowlights in the hollows of their cheeks (suck in your cheeks and you will see the hollows), down the sides of their nose, along the jawbone and under the chin.

Skeleton

Follow basic makeup steps #1 through #3 on page 113, EXCEPT …

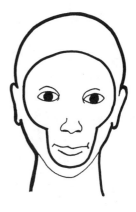

1. Use white makeup for the base and apply it to only the center of the face. Powder.

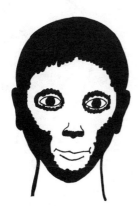

2. Darken the eye area, end of the nose, around the nostrils and the outside of the face using black.

3. Use a makeup brush to define the skeleton outline with white makeup. Powder.

4. Use a makeup brush to define the eyes and nose in black. Add the skeleton's mouth by drawing around the outside of the mouth. Draw a line side to side, using the space where the lips meet as the separation line. Add teeth. Powder.

Clown Face
Follow basic makeup steps #1 through #3 on page 113, EXCEPT ...

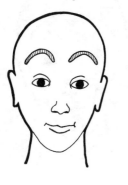

1. Use white makeup for the entire base.

2. Draw some crazy eyebrows, using any color. Outline with liner. Powder.

3. Use any color eyeshadow, to fill in from the eyelid to the crazy eyebrow.

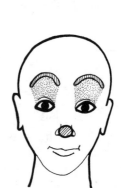

4. Outline eyes. Powder. Add mascara to eyelashes, if desired.

5. Color the end of nose. Outline and powder.

6. Add a big smile, outline, and powder.

TIP: Because clown makeup is traditionally done with a white makeup base, it is especially important that you keep your brushes, hands and makeup area very clean, as white base can get very dirty.

Cat Face

Follow basic makeup steps #1 through #3 on page 113, EXCEPT …

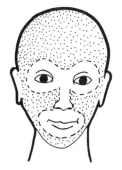

1. Use the main color for your cat around the outer areas of the face, leaving the center area clear. Powder.

2. Sponge white makeup onto the center of the face. Powder.

3. Use a makeup brush to create white "fur" by making short strokes over white sponged area. Powder.

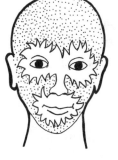

4. Outline eyes in a dark color. Powder.

5. Add nose, nose line from under nose to top of lip, whisker dots above upper lip, and whiskers with a dark color. Powder.

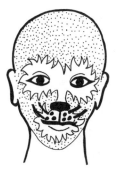

6. Add stripes all around the outside of the face in different colors. Powder.

MAKEUP REMOVAL: Taking off your makeup can sometimes be as much work as putting it on. If you are using water-based makeup, begin by gently wiping your face off with a babywipe towel. Follow by washing with soap and water. If you are trying to remove greasepaint, rub a little bit of petroleum jelly over your skin first. Then, use the babywipe to remove the makeup. Follow by washing with soap and water.

Actors' Roles

Every show has different parts to be performed by actors, singers, dancers or whatever type of talent is required to make that particular performance work. These parts, which might be individual characters or multiple roles to be played by the same person, will need to be **CAST**, or filled, to make the actual performance happen.

In order to cast these roles, you may need to hold an **AUDITION**. An audition is when people who want to be in a show read for a part. In other words, the people auditioning would read selected lines from the script for a particular character from that show. If it is a musical, everyone would also need to sing and dance. Then the director (choreographer and musical director, if is a musical) will decide who to cast (put) into the show.

You may have several parts that are **PRE-CAST**. This means that some of the roles have already been promised to certain actors prior to the auditions.

Practice Makes Perfect

After the final casting has taken place, you will need to put together a **REHEARSAL SCHEDULE**. This will be the time when everyone meets and rehearses (practices and works on) the show.

You can organize as few or as many rehearsals as you need. The reason to hold rehearsals is so everyone has the opportunity to learn their parts and can work with the other actors to know what they will be doing on the stage through movement, character and motivation. It also gives the director time to set (decide on) what **BLOCKING** will be used by the actors. Blocking is the name used to refer to movement on the stage for both actors and crew members who are arranging set pieces and props during the performance. If the director asked you to **CROSS** (move from one place to another) toward a certain character during a line, that is part of the blocking you will be given for that particular scene.

Stage direction is divided up into the nine different blocks as discussed in WHAT IS A STAGE? on page 22. So, as you are moving across the stage, you are technically moving from block to block ... in other words, blocking your moves!

WHAT IS A REHEARSAL?

What Every Actor Should Know for Rehearsal

REHEARSAL is the time when you learn your part, memorize your lines and try out your costumes and makeup. In other words, it is the time you use to prepare for your performance before the audience.

Your **SCRIPT** is the book, notebook or papers that contains the lines, directions and background information about the show. A responsible actor should always have a sharpened pencil at rehearsal so information can be marked (written down) such as blocking and special notes that should be remembered.

BLOCKING is all the movement you do for the show. You may be asked to go upstage, downstage, toward stage right or stage left. You may also have to make a cross which means to move from one area of the stage to another during a scene.

	UPSTAGE	
UPSTAGE RIGHT	UPSTAGE CENTER	UPSTAGE LEFT
RIGHT CROSS →	CENTER	LEFT
DOWNSTAGE RIGHT	DOWNSTAGE CENTER	DOWNSTAGE LEFT

STAGE RIGHT — DOWNSTAGE — STAGE LEFT

HUNTER: WOW, MITCHELL. THAT PUMPKIN SURE WAS FAST!

MITCHELL: GOOD THING GRANDPA HAD PARKED THE MOTORHOME RIGHT THERE TO STOP IT!

LINES are the sentences spoken by the characters in the script. Sometimes, during rehearsals, you may be asked to **RUN LINES**. That means to practice reading your lines with another actor in an effort to memorize.

TO ENTER means you are coming onto the stage area from off stage. You can **MAKE AN ENTRANCE** from stage right, the right side of the stage as you face the audience, or from stage left, the left side of the stage as you face the audience. You may even be directed to enter through The House, meaning you would be coming through the audience from the back of the theatre. **TO EXIT** means you are leaving the stage area.

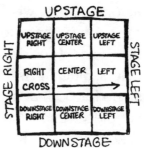

To **MOVE DOWNSTAGE** of someone means you should cross in front of the other person or people with whom you are doing the scene, so you are closest to the audience. To **MOVE UPSTAGE** of someone means that you cross behind the other person, so you are furthest away from the audience.

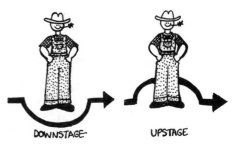

CUT = STOP
PICK UP = GO

If the director says **CUT**, he is asking the actors to stop the scene. He may want to give a **NOTE**, which is a change or correction. When the information has been given and/or the changes have been made, the director will ask the actors to **PICK-UP** (continue with) the scene where it had been stopped.

To **HOLD FOR APPLAUSE** or "laughs" means that the audience may want to applaud (clap their hands) or laugh after something special has happened, such as a musical number or a great joke. By **HOLDING,** the actors do not continue on with the scene until most of the applause or laughter has almost finished. By doing this, the audience will not miss any of the lines in the performance.

PROJECTING YOUR VOICE means to speak loudly and clearly so that the audience can hear you, with or without the use of microphones. **DICTION,** speaking your words very clearly and understandably, is also extremely important to projection.

SHHHH!

A **STAGE WHISPER** is an exaggerated whisper done by using your voice in a hushed (quiet) manner so the audience can understand that you are whispering, but also hear what you are saying.

An **ACCENT**, sometimes called a **DIALECT**, is a way of speaking that indicates through your speech that you are from a particular country or region. For example, someone who comes from Ireland is said to have an Irish accent, just as people who come from the Southern United States may be said to have a Southern accent. For some characters, the use of an accent is very important to the development of their role and would be a distinctive character trait.

CHARACTER TRAITS are the distinctive ways a character walks, talks and possibly even sneezes. If you have the opportunity to observe people, such as in a library or at the supermarket, you will notice some of the little things they do. Some people scratch their heads when they talk, twist their hair into ringlets, have a really funny laugh or limp when they walk. These are **UNCONSCIOUS MOVEMENTS** (meaning the people do not realize they are doing them). Everybody does them. It can make stage characters appear more **REALISTIC** (life-like) if you give them one or two of these types of traits. They are also sometimes known as **PHYSICAL CHARACTERIZATIONS** because they have to do with how you use your body when playing your character.

STAGE BUSINESS refers to all the little things a character might do while talking to someone, waiting for another character to arrive or when generally involved in a scene in some aspect. Picking up a magazine, dusting off furniture or peeling a banana are all bits of stage business. They are the little things someone would normally do to pass time in any given situation.

CHARACTERIZATION means the development, through rehearsal of the role (character) being portrayed (played). For example, if the role you are working on is a pirate, depending on the surrounding circumstances, most likely you would act quite differently from playing the part of a school teacher. Another major part of characterization is the emotional state of your character such as happy, sad, in love, angry or upset with another character. Just as you have feelings and emotions, so does your character. That is what can make acting so much fun and such a great challenge. You get to create someone entirely from your own imagination.

Now you can start **GETTING INTO CHARACTER.** That is when you take all the bits and pieces you have developed and convincingly step into and become (act like) the role you are playing.

The Actor's Secret

1. **Learn the power of observation.** By watching the people around you, you can learn lots of wonderful things about how people act. Watch people walk. Eat their food. Blow their noses. It is all of those little things we have a tendency to overlook in our everyday living that a good actor knows are the secrets to making a character come to life on stage.

2. **Learn to listen.** Close your eyes and listen to all of the sounds around you. Listen to the different vocal patterns people use: their accents, their vocabulary. Listen to their voices, the pitch and the tempo. Listen to birds, cars and vacuum cleaners. Noises add a tremendous amount of depth to a performance because everything has its own sound. Listening helps all of us to understand one another and communicate better. A good actor knows that when we listen, we think, and when we think, we can answer and respond clearly.

3. **Believe in your dreams.** Everybody's heart is full of dreams and wishes. A good actor will follow his dreams wherever they may lead him. Dreams make each one of us the special individuals we are.

Actors, Take Your Places

As you can see, there are many different aspects to putting on a show. You don't need lots of fancy things to make your show great —just good ideas, energy, a positive attitude and creativity.

One of the best things you can do in getting ready for a show is to be organized when putting together the production. Here is a checklist of some things you may want to think about:

SHOW (what kind of show shall we do?)

PEOPLE (who will be in it?)

PLACE (where to do it?)

SETS (do we need sets?)

COSTUMES (what shall we wear?)

PROPS (are we going to use props?)

DAY and TIME (when are we going to do it?)

REHEARSALS (are we going to practice and, if so, how often and where?)

Some of these areas will be very easy to coordinate and you may already have them covered. But whether you have the answers to begin with or not, it is important to think about your overall plan because good preparation will have a positive effect on your show.

Getting Organized

Little reminders to help you get ready for putting on your own show.

1. What type of show would you like to present? A play you wrote yourself, one borrowed from the library, a musical review featuring a variety of singing and dancing numbers, a series of skits or an impromptu performance. If you want to do something with your friends, talk to all of them, too. Everybody has great ideas, so share. It will be  more exciting, fun and productive to work together. For a complete catalog of plays that will fit many of your needs contact Meriwether Publishing Ltd. - Contemporary Drama Service, 885 Elkton Drive, Colorado Springs, CO 80907, phone: (719) 594-4422 or visit their website: www.contemporarydrama.com.

2. Who will be assigned what responsibilities for the show? You will need a director and someone to be in charge of building the sets. Who is interested in being an actor or stage manager? The best way to do your own show is by involving everyone in several different areas. Everyone can act in the show, help make the sets, find costumes, even fold programs and serve refreshments! Group effort toward a single goal can make for a successful production because everyone will take pride in his or her collective work.

3. Where are you able to do your show? At your house, school, in a garage or even outside. There are many great places you can use! Remember that you also have the resources to be able to make your own stage and curtain. So, you can put on your show just about anywhere!

4. What date and what time are you going to do your show? You need to make certain that the place you would like to use will be available. You must also make certain that your cast and crew will be available for the performance date, too.

5. Are you planning on using a set and, if so, are you going to design and build it, borrow parts of it or a combination of both? Depending on where you are planning on presenting your show, you may not need to have a set, only set pieces.

6. Do you need costumes and props? Maybe you have some old Halloween outfits or clothing you can use? What about borrowing some items to use for props? How many costumes and props are you able to create on your own?

7. Are you going to have rehearsals? Have you picked a place to hold them? Just like with finding a place to do your show, most rehearsals can be done just about anywhere! You must also consider what times and dates your rehearsals will be held.

8. Have you thought about having programs or refreshments for your audience? Will you be arranging some sort of publicity in the form of flyers or local newspaper articles so all your friends and the local community will know about your show? Those are also things you may want to consider.

These are just some helpful reminders, but above all else, the most important thing is to just have fun!

Butterflies in Your Stomach

So now the time has come to just go out on stage and have some fun! The rehearsals are all done. The actors have all memorized their lines and are anxiously waiting in the wings for their entrances. The costumes are ready. The sets are in place. Everybody has **BUTTERFLIES IN THEIR STOMACH**, which is just a little pre-performance jitters or nervousness and all part of putting on a show.

If you listen closely, you can hear the audience is just as excited as you are for the show to begin. The last bit of advice? Enjoy yourself and **BREAK A LEG**.

Don't worry about really breaking a leg. That is what someone says to you before your opening performance. "Break a leg" really means good luck, because there is a superstition in theatre that it is bad luck to wish someone good luck on their opening night and good luck to wish them the opposite sentiment.

Last-Minute Tips and the Big Finale

This is what an appreciative audience will give at the end of the show to everyone, cast and crew, who has worked so hard. You deserve it! So go out there and take your bows!

One of the most magical things about the theatre is that when the show is all over and the audience has left, everything is cleaned up, and it looks as if a show had never been there.

BREAKDOWN, or "breaking down the show," is when everything is returned to its proper place. All the costumes are re-hung. The props and sets are stored. Everything that was borrowed is returned in good condition. The theatre or area in which the performance has taken place is swept, straightened up and all the trash removed and thrown away. As if by magic, it will look as if no one had ever set foot on the stage.

Even better, if you demonstrate responsibility in the use of any facilities, properties or equipment, people will be very happy to help you the next time you want to do a production. Courtesy, kindness and consideration are as valuable a tool for anyone involved in the theatre, not to mention in "real life," as putting on a good performance.

One More Thing . . .

Doing your own show can be lots of fun and very exciting. You may find out that you really enjoy writing stories and seeing them done on the stage. You may discover that you have a gift for acting, singing and/or dancing. You may find that you really enjoy designing and creating costumes, building sets or inventing props out of funny bits and pieces someone else might have thrown away. Or you may like making flyers, posters, and creating programs. There are lots of different opportunities and experiences you can be involved with in the theatre and every one is equally important and special. Always remember, theatre is a gift to be shared and enjoyed.

I hope this book has helped you learn more about some of the basics in theatre and how to put on your own show. So, remember, the next time there is a rainy day or you think you have nothing to do, open this book and let your creativity fill the time. Rain or shine, any day is a great day to use your imagination and experience the wonder that is theatre!

Good Luck

Or as we say on opening nights . . .

"Break A Leg!"

Theatre Glossary

A.D.	Short for ASSISTANT DIRECTOR.
A.I.	Short for ACT ONE. See Act One.
AII	Short for ACT TWO. See Act Two.
ACCENT	Way of talking that can indicate where someone is from, sometimes also called a DIALECT.
ACCESSORY	Something added to a costume- shoes, socks, hats, eyeglasses, purses, etc.
ACCOUNT FOR	To explain.
ACKNOWLEDGE	Letting people know that someone helped or did something kind.
ACROBAT	Someone who performs gymnastics.
ACROBATICS	Gymnastic tricks like tumbling.
ACT	To pretend to be a person, animal, or object for a performance; also, a grouping of scenes in a play or musical.
ACT ONE	The grouping of scenes that make up the first half of a play or musical.
ACT TWO	The grouping of scenes that make up the second half of a play or musical.
ACTING COMPANY	Group of performers that have established a repertoire and work together on a regular basis. See ACTING TROUPE.
ACTING TROUPE	Group of performers that have established a repertoire and work together on a regular basis. See ACTING COMPANY.
ACTION	Any kind of movement, from a nose wiggle to running.
ACTOR	Person who pretends to be a person, animal, or object, often in a play or musical.
ADAPTATION	When a play is based upon another story.
ADJUST	To make appropriate for the situation so it works.
ALLOWANCE	Amount permitted.
ALWAYS	To do every time, be consistent.

APPLAUD	Showing appreciation or support by clapping hands together at a quick rate.
APPLY	To put on.
ARABIC NUMBERS	Numbers we see in every day use: 1, 2, 3, 4, etc.
ARRANGEMENT	To make plans or organize; also, the way a musical director organizes some music for a performance.
ARENA	Flat area in center of stadium.
ASPECT	Certain area or portion.
ASSISTANT DIRECTOR	Person who helps the director in putting on the show.
AUDIBLE	To be heard.
AUDIENCE	People who see a show.
AUDIO	Sound.
AUDIO DESIGNER	Person who decides about all the sound needs for a show also called SOUND DESIGNER.
AUDIO EQUIPMENT	Machines, electronics, cables and cords, anything that helps to produce sound for a show, same as SOUND EQUIPMENT.
AUDIO SYSTEM	How all the audio/sound equipment is organized to produce sound for the show, same as SOUND SYSTEM.
AUDITION	Process by which people are selected for parts in a show, often through acting, singing and dancing.
AUTHOR/PLAYWRIGHT	Person who has written a play.
AVAILABLE	Something that is not being used.
BABYWIPE TOWEL	Wet cloth in a pop-up container, often used to clean up babies.
BACKDROP	Curtain that hangs at the back of the stage, often depicting landscape.
BACKGROUND INFORMATION	Information that may not be told in the story, but could provide explanation to the present situation.
BACKGROUND MUSIC	Music that provides additional depth to a scene, may or may not be significant to the story.
BACKSTAGE	Area behind or off the sides of the stage where the audience cannot see the actors or crew.
BALANCE	Everything is even and equal on both sides.
BALLET	Classical form of dance.
BAND	Group of musicians playing together, usually without stringed instruments.

BAR	In music, a segment of notes, also called a MEASURE.
BASE	Wide/heavy enough to keep something balanced, usually at the bottom; also, the first part applied in makeup.
BASED UPON	Where the original idea came from (adapted from).
BASIC	The simplest form, what everything else comes from or is built upon.
BEGIN	To start.
BEGINING	Where something starts.
BEHIND THE SCENES	Everything that happens to make a show work and what goes on during a show that the audience cannot see.
BELIEVE	To want to make true or real.
BELONGINGS	Personal items.
BIG TOP	Name given to circus tent.
BLACK LIGHTS	Lights that make white and fluorescent and neon colors stand out in the dark.
BLOCKING	To stand or move to a certain position on stage as instructed, also called STAGE DIRECTION or STAGING.
BLUSHER	Colored powder makeup that is applied to cheeks.
BOBBY PINS	Hair pins, used to hold hair and wigs in desired position.
BODY MICROPHONE	Microphone that is worn directly on the body, also called body mic.
BOOK	To schedule a location or hire actors for performance; also, another word for SCRIPT.
BOOMBOX	Large portable radio, sometimes also a tape recorder and player.
BORROW	To use something that belongs to someone else with the intent of returning it safely and in good condition.
BOW	Low bend at the waist used to acknowledge the audience's appreciation, some women prefer to CURTSEY instead.
BRAD	Small metal clasp used to hold together papers.
BREAK A LEG	Said to performers on opening night instead of good luck, based on superstition.
BREAKDOWN	To take apart and put away.
BREAKING CHARACTER	When an actor suddenly becomes himself, instead of the character he is playing, on stage by laughing or forgetting a line.

BREAKING DOWN A SHOW	To take apart and put away everything that has to do with a show.
BREAKING THE FOURTH WALL	When actors walk through the invisible wall dividing the stage area from the audience and continue the performance in the House.
BUILD	To make something, also CONSTRUCT.
BUSINESS	Short for STAGE BUSINESS.
BUTTERFLIES IN YOUR STOMACH	An expression meaning to feel very nervous.
CAKE	Flat container holding hard-pressed makeup.
CALL THE SHOW	What the stage manager does when he gives cues during a show.
CALLS	Instructions given by the stage manager to the crew.
CAST	All of the performers in the show; also, to give actors parts in a show.
CAST OF CHARACTERS	All of the roles/parts in a show, usually listed in the program.
CATEGORY	A specific group of things or ideas.
CELEBRATE	Enjoy with great enthusiasm.
CENTER	The middle.
CENTER STAGE	In the middle of the stage.
CENTRAL	The middle point, around which other things happen.
CHALLENGE	To try for something that may be a little more work and effort.
CHARACTER	A part or role in a play; also, the kind of person someone is.
CHARACTERISTICS	Physical features or habits.
CHARACTERIZATION	Creating a personality for a character including the way they walk, speak and think.
CHARACTER NAME	The name of an actor's part in the show.
CHARACTER TRAIT	Little habits or activities that make a character special and adds personality, same as PHYSICAL TRAIT.
CHARLESTON	Popular dance from the 1920s.
CHARTED	Written down in a format that indicates placement of certain property.
CHECKLIST	List of everything to do.
CHOREOGRAPHER	Person who makes up and teaches all dances, fights or movements for a musical or play.

CHOREOGRAPHY	Name for all the dance steps used in a musical.
CHORUS	Group of performers that support the lead players in a show, sometimes called the ENSEMBLE.
CHRONOLOGICAL	In the order of what time things happened.
CIRCUS	Often a traveling show that features animals, acrobats, clowns and daredevils. Usually performed in a ring.
CLASSICAL	Very old style and form, often considered the basis for other forms.
CLASSIFY	Identify by characteristics.
CLEAN UP	To pick up and clear away everything from the area; also to fix sections of a show that need work through rehearsal.
CLOWN	Person who is a funny entertainer, often wearing special makeup and best known for appearing in the circus.
COLLABORATION	When two or more people work together on a project.
COLLECTION	Grouping of items with something in common.
COLON	Punctuation mark used to separate ideas in a sentence.
COMEDY	Funny story or situation created to make people laugh.
COMIC	A funny character, often a slapstick performer.
COMPOSITION	Either a story or music.
CONCEPT	The overall idea behind a project.
CONDUCTOR	Person who leads the orchestra and singers in their songs during a performance.
CONFIGURATION	How things are organized.
CONFLICT	Difference of ideas.
CONSIDERATE	Being thoughtful, thinking about someone else first before yourself.
CONSTRUCT	To make, build or put something together.
CONSTRUCTION	Act of building, making or putting something together.
CONTRAST	Different from something else in color, texture, size or the like.
COORDINATE	To organize so everything works together.
COSTUME	Clothing an actor wears during a show.
COSTUME DESIGNER	Person who creates and builds the costumes for a show.
COTTON SWAB	Small stick with a tiny bit of cotton on each end, used to clean ears and for makeup application and correction.

COUNTRY MUSIC	Music that is based on folk songs, sometimes thought of as cowboy music.
COURTESY	Being polite.
CREATE	To make up, imagine, dream or invent something.
CREATIVE	To be inventive in making up ways of doing things.
CREATIVITY	A climate of new ideas, being creative.
CREDIT	To let others know who originally had the idea.
CREW	Group of people who work backstage.
CROSS	To move to another person or to an object on stage.
CUE	To let someone know at a specific time to do something with regard to the show.
CULTURE	Stories, skills, arts and crafts, songs and dances that are special to a certain group of people who share a common history and/or background.
CURTAIN	Large piece of fabric that opens and closes across the front of the stage, separating the actors from the audience.
CURTSEY	Ladies bow with one leg crossed behind the other, both knees bend slightly, and the head nods forward in acknowledgment of applause.
CUT	To slice something into portions using a sharpened object; also, what a director might say to stop a scene from continuing.
DANCE	Movement of the body, usually to music.
DAREDEVIL	Person who does wild stunts.
DECK	Floor area of the stage, usually wooden, also called FLOORBOARDS.
DECK CREW	Group that works in the backstage area during a show, also called the RUNNING CREW.
DEFINED	Explained.
DEFINITION	What something means as in a phrase, word or action.
DELIVERY	Way a spoken line is presented in a play.
DERIVATIVE	Taken from a specific source.
DESCRIBE	To tell how something looks, feels, tastes, sounds or smells.
DESIGNER	Person who creates something special for a project.
DIAGRAM	To demonstrate how something may look using pictures or objects.

DIALECT	Specific way of speaking that can indicate where someone is from, also called an ACCENT.
DIALOG	Two or more people speaking to one another on stage.
DICTION	Clear and precise use of language where every vowel and consonant can be heard. See ENUNCIATION.
DIRECTOR	Person who works with the designers and actors and is in charge of the creative aspects of the show.
DIRECTIONAL	Words in the script, usually in parentheses, that tell an actor of any special movement or emotion that goes with a line.
DIRECTION	What a director will give an actor in rehearsal.
DISPLAY	To show something.
DISTINCTIVE	Having unusual and/or unique qualities.
DOWNSTAGE	Area closest to the audience, at the front of the stage.
DRAMA	Serious story or situation.
DRAMATIC	Acting in a serious manner.
DRESS REHEARSAL	Practice wearing all costumes and makeup and using all sets and props. Usually done one or two days prior to opening night.
DUPLICATED	Copied.
DURATION	Length of time.
EDIT	Cutting the script to make it more efficient and/or effective.
EFFECT	Something done to create a certain idea or image.
ELEMENT	An important part or piece of something that makes up a whole product.
EMOTION	Feelings.
END	To finish.
ENDING	When or where something finishes.
ENUNCIATION	Clear, well-pronounced words, where all the vowels and consonants can be heard, also called DICTION.
ENSEMBLE	The collective name for a cast of performers; can also refer to CHORUS members.
ENTERTAINER	Person who performs in front of people.
ENTRANCE	When an actor comes out onto the stage.
ENVIRONMENT	Surroundings.

ESTABLISH	To set up or prove.
EVENT	Usually something big that is planned or expected to happen.
EXIT	When an actor leaves the stage.
EXPERIMENT	To try something new and see what happens.
EYEBROW PENCIL	Makeup pencil used to make eyebrows darker.
EYELINER	Makeup pencil or liquid used to outline eyes.
EYESHADOW	Colored powder applied to eyelids and sometimes around the eye.
FABLE	Fictional story, often featuring animals, that teaches moral lesson.
FABRIC	Material used to make costumes.
FAIRY TALE	Fictional story usually about magical deeds.
FAMILIAR	Something that you know and understand very well.
FEATURE	Identifying part of the face of body; also special section of show spotlighting an actor, usually in song or dance.
FEATURED PLAYER	Performer who has a special song or character in a show, but is not a lead or supporting player.
FICTION	Story that has been made up and is not true.
FINGER PUPPET	Small doll worn over fingertip.
FLAT	Part of the set that can be painted to represent many different things.
FLOOR MICROPHONE	Microphone that is set on the floor, usually at the front of the stage, also called floor mic.
FLOORBOARDS	Floor area of the stage, usually wooden, also called the DECK.
FLUORESCENT	Color so bright that it can almost be seen in the dark. See NEON.
FLUSH	Pushed up smoothly against something else, as if it were all one piece.
FLY	Short for FLY GALLERY.
FLY GALLERY	Open spaced area above the stage where scenery can be stored out of view from the audience.
FLY IN	When a piece of scenery is lowered to the stage.
FLY OUT	When a piece of scenery is raised from the stage.
FLY SPACE	Another name for the FLY GALLERY.
FOCUS	To make clear.

FOLK DANCE/SONG	Traditional, cultural dances and songs.
FOLKLORE	Traditional stories and beliefs of a family, village, town, city, state, region or country.
FOOTLIGHTS	Lights that are set up across the front of the stage, usually in a strip.
FORMAL	Proper.
FORMAT	How something is set up and organized.
FOURTH WALL	Invisible wall that separates the audience from the actors on stage.
FRAME	Structure over which cloth is stretched to create a flat.
FREE-STANDING	Able to stand alone.
FULL-LENGTH	Standard performance time without cuts.
FULL-SIZED PUPPET	Doll that puppeteer stands inside of to move, sometimes called a costume character.
FUNKY CHICKEN	Silly dance from the 1960s.
GELS	Special colored film that can be placed over lights to create different colors.
GENRE	A specific type of art or literature.
GETTING INTO CHARACTER	When an actor pretends to become the character they are playing.
GLOSSARY	Collection of definitions found at the back of a book.
GOBO	Special metal plate that slides over lights to create interesting shapes and designs on the stage.
GOOD LUCK	To wish for someone that nice things will happen to and for them.
GREASEPAINT	Stage makeup that has a greasy feel.
GRID	Poles attached to the ceiling from which lighting and sound equipment is hung.
GROUNDLING	Someone from the early days of theater who stood on the ground to watch performances, the least expensive admission.
HAND PUPPET	Doll worn over the hand.
HAND-HELD MICROPHONE	Microphone that is held in the hand during performance, also called hand-held mic.
HANG	How lights and sound equipment are placed up on the grid.

HIGH-WIRE ARTIST	Performer who works on a tightrope, usually in the circus, also called TIGHTROPE WALKER.
HIGHLIGHT	When a lighter shade of makeup is applied so a certain area of the face is noticed.
HISTORICAL TIME	From past to present.
HISTORY	Things that have happened in the past.
HOLD	To wait.
HOLD FOR APPLAUSE	To wait for the audience to almost stop clapping their hands before going on with the scene.
HOLD FOR LAUGHS	To wait for the audience to almost stop laughing before going on with the scene.
HOLLOWS	Portion of cheek that is under the cheekbone and above jawline that is slightly indented.
HOUSE	Where the audience sits.
HUMOROUS	Something funny.
HUSH	Quiet, but still able to be heard.
HYDRAULIC	Technical system that uses the power of water to move heavy set pieces.
IDEA	When someone's imagination thinks of something to do or make.
IDENTIFY	To recognize.
IDIOSYNCRASY	Quirk, odd habit, peculiar behavior.
ILLUMINATE	To light, lighten or brighten.
ILLUSION	Magic trick; also, something that looks to be real, but is not.
ILLUSTRATE	To show something by drawing a picture of it.
IMAGINATION	Making up a picture in your mind.
IMAGINE	To picture something in your mind.
IMPORTANT	Having great meaning.
IMPROVISATION	Something done on the spur of the moment that comes instantly to your mind, also called IMPROV.
IMPROVISE	To make something up instantly.
IN PLACE	When an actor is in position for an entrance or the beginning of a scene.
IN THE ROUND	Theatre in which the audience sits on all sides and the actors perform in the middle.

INDENTED	Bent inward or set back.
INDIVIDUAL	One person.
INFRARED SOUND SYSTEM	Special hearing device that uses invisible infrared sound waves to transport sound to people who cannot hear very well.
INSIGNIFICANT	Having little or no importance to the situation.
INSTANTANEOUSLY	At that exact moment.
INSTRUCT	Explain how to do, also see DIRECT.
INSTRUCTION	To explain how to do something, also see DIRECTION.
INSTRUMENTS	Objects used to create music.
INTERACTIVE	Involve the audience in the performance.
INTERMISSION	Break between the acts of a play or musical.
INTRIGUE	Secret plot, suspense.
INVENT	To create something, usually to solve a problem.
INVENTION	A created device that solves a problem.
JAZZ	Short for JAZZ DANCE or JAZZ MUSIC; also, a way of speaking in slang.
JAZZ DANCE	Dance style that is performed to jazz music.
JAZZ MUSIC	Music that is syncopated in style.
JITTERBUG	Fast, acrobatic dance for couples from the 1940s.
JOIN	Come or bring together.
KINDNESS	Being nice to others.
LEAD	To direct an orchestra, band and/or singers in rehearsal or performance; also, short for LEADING LADY, LEADING MAN, and LEADING PLAYER.
LEADING LADY	Primary female character in the story, also called a PRINCIPAL or STAR.
LEADING MAN	Primary male character in the story, also called a PRINCIPAL or STAR.
LEADING PLAYER	Primary character of the story, also called a PRINCIPAL or STAR.
LEGEND	Story passed on from generation to generation, usually about historic deeds or to explain certain occurrences and happenings.

LEGS	Long curtains that hang in the wings to hide actors from the audience before entrances.
LEVEL	Flat and even, smooth.
LIBRARIAN	Person who works in a library and can assist in finding information.
LIBRARY	Place with a large collection of books, records and other information.
LIGHT	A source of illumination that allows one to see in a darkened area.
LIGHTING CHART	Drawn layout of how the lights will be hung, same as LIGHTING PLOT.
LIGHTING CREW	Group that assists in all of the work done with the lighting for a show.
LIGHTING DESIGNER	Person who decides where the lights must be hung and what special gels, gobos or effects are needed for the show.
LIGHTING EFFECTS	Changing the lights to give them a different look.
LIGHTING PLOT	Drawn layout of how the lights will be hung, same as LIGHTING CHART.
LINE	Words in the script spoken by the characters.
LIPLINER	Special makeup pen or pencil used for outlining lips.
LIPSTICK	Colored makeup that goes on lips, usually in a tube or pot.
WEARING LOTS OF HATS	When someone does more than one thing at a time.
LOWLIGHT	When a darker shade of makeup is applied so a certain area of the face is not noticed.
LYRICS	Words used when singing a song.
M.D.	Short for MUSICAL DIRECTOR.
MAGICIAN	Person who performs illusions and magic tricks.
MAKE AN ENTRANCE	When an actor comes out onto the stage.
MAKE AN EXIT	When an actor leaves the stage.
MAKE-BELIEVE	To create imaginary events.
MAKEUP	Applied to the face to assist and sometimes alter appearance.
MAKEUP BRUSH	Special brush to be used only for applying makeup.
MAKEUP DESIGNER	Person who creates makeup for a show.
MAKEUP KIT	Variety of makeup products that come in a single package.

MAKEUP POT	Small round containers that hold powder or gel makeup.
MAKEUP REMOVAL	Taking off makeup.
MAKEUP STICK	Tube of makeup, usually greasepaint.
MAKING A CHARACTER COME TO LIFE	Acting so well that the character seems to be real.
MANIPULATE	To handle in such a manner that the situation works out in a particular way.
MARIONETTES	Puppets with strings.
MARK	To write down a cue or note in your script; also, to walk through your blocking from memory.
MASCARA	Makeup applied to darken eyelashes.
MATERIAL	Supplies gathered to make something; also, fabric for costumes.
MEANING	What a word or phrase stands for or represents.
MEASURE	To figure out the size of something; also, in music, a segment of notes, sometimes also called a BAR.
MELODRAMA	Popular old-style play that is over-acted, where the audience participates by cheering, booing and hissing.
MEMORIZE	To be able to remember something without having to look at notes, lines or reminders.
MICROPHONE	Electronic device that helps to make sounds louder.
MICROPHONE STAND	Pole designed to hold a microphone.
MIDDLE	Center; also, between other objects.
MIME	Person who performs mime or pantomime.
MINIMAL	Limited in number, size or length.
MIX	To blend together all the sounds.
MODERN DANCE	Dance style that is freer and less structured.
MOMENT	A little bit of time, not really any specified length.
MONITOR	Speakers on stage through which performers can hear the music, sound effects and each other during the show.
MONOLOG	Long speech by one person, soliloquy.
MORAL	Lesson to be learned and lived by.
MORALISTIC	Behavior attributed to living a certain set of ethical rules, usually based on a society's standards.
MOTIVATION	Reason why someone behaves or responds in a certain manner based on previous circumstances or ideas.

MOVE	Any kind of motion that takes you from one place to another.
MOVEMENT	Any kind of motion.
MUSIC	Rhythmic or melodic sounds linked together.
MUSICAL	Play that tells the story through singing and dancing.
MUSICAL DIRECTOR	Person who teaches all the music to the orchestra and cast.
MUSICAL NUMBER	Song performed in a show.
MUSICIANS	Performers who play instruments.
MYSTERY	Something that makes you wonder or curious.
MYSTERIOUS	Situation or person that makes you wonder or curious.
NEAT	Clean, everything in place.
NEAT AND TIDY	Everywhere and everything is cleaned, picked-up and put into the proper place.
NEON	Color so bright that is can almost be seen in the dark. See FLUORESCENT.
NON-FICTION	Story that is true, or true information.
NORMALLY	As things are everyday.
NOTE	Correction or change given by the director or other production team member; also, the marking used to write music.
NUMBER	Short for MUSICAL NUMBER.
OBSERVATION	Watching carefully what is happening all around.
ONE ACT PLAY	Play that has the beginning, middle and ending in several scenes, but not long enough to have an intermission.
ONE PERSON SHOW	Performance featuring only one person, sometimes called SOLO ACT.
ON STAGE	Being in front of an audience.
OPENING NIGHT	First night of a show in front of an audience.
OPERA	Similar to a musical, but performed with classical music.
ORCHESTRA	Group of musicians who perform together.
ORGANIZE	To put things into order.
ORIGINAL	Brand new idea or thought no one else has ever had before.
OVER-ACTING	When an actor is making all of his movements, emotions, and activity much too big, exaggerated.

OVERTONES	When an idea or situation has an effect on another idea or situation.
PANTOMIME	Performance done without talking, often without set and props, as well. See also MIME.
PARENTHESIS	Curved lines that enclose a directional action.
PART	Character in a play, also called a ROLE.
PAST	Anything that happened earlier.
PERIOD PIECE	Show that is set in a particular time period and requiring specific settings, props and costumes among other elements.
PERFORM	To appear in front of an audience and do a show.
PERFORMER	Person who appears before an audience and does a show.
PERFORMANCE	To do a show.
PERMISSION	Asking if something is okay to do, take or use.
PERSONALITY	Qualities that make each person an individual, different.
PETROLEUM JELLY	Greasy substance used for taking off makeup.
PICK-UP	To begin a scene again where it left off.
PIECE	Part of a whole object.
PIVOTAL	Turning point, a center from which things radiate.
PHYSICAL	Having to do with the body.
PHYSICAL TRAIT	Little habits or activities that make a character special and add personality, same as CHARACTER TRAIT.
PLACEMENT	Where something is put.
PLAN	To organize, coordinate so everything works together.
PLAY	Show consisting of lines that are all spoken.
PLAY A PART	To be a character in a show.
PLAY ACTING	Trying out some ideas through acting; also sometimes known as ROLE PLAYING.
PLAYED OUT	How something worked in a particular situation.
PLAYER	Another name for an actor.
PLAYWRIGHT	Person who writes a play.
PLAYWRITING	To compose or write a play.
PLOT	How a story goes from beginning to middle to end, same as STORYLINE.

POLITE	To have good manners and behavior.
POPULAR	Current favorite of everybody.
POPULAR DANCE	Current favorite dance of everybody.
POPULAR MUSIC	Current favorite music of everybody, also called POP MUSIC.
PORTABLE	Easily movable.
PORTRAY	To play a role, often associated with non-fictional characters.
POWER	Strength.
POWDER	Soft, loose substance, that is put on makeup to keep it from coming off.
POWDER PUFF	Soft, flat, round pad used for applying powder to makeup.
PRINCIPAL	Person about whom the story of the show is all about, also called a LEADING PLAYER or STAR.
PRACTICE	To do over and over and over again until you have it the way you want it to be, see REHEARSAL.
PREMISE	Basis for reasoning or idea.
PRESENT	To show something to someone.
PRESENT TIME	Right now, at this moment.
PRESENTATION	Show usually featuring one item as the center of attention such as a new car or an award.
PRETEND	To imagine and play as if you are someone or something different or in a different place.
PRIMARY	Of first importance.
PRIORITY	Of greatest importance, sequence of importance.
PRODUCTION	Show, sometimes considered to be a very large show with lots of people.
PRODUCTION TEAM	Group who makes decisions about the show, such as all the directors and designers.
PROFESSIONAL	Person who gets paid for doing a job.
PROFESSIONAL THEATRE	Theatre performances where everyone working on the show gets paid.
PROGRAM	Order of events as they occur in a show; also, brochure or flyer audience receives filled with cast and show information.
PROJECT	Job you or someone else gives you to do, also, speaking with a good, strong voice to be heard.
PROJECTED IMAGES	Anything that puts light and design onto the stage, using movie, video or slide projectors.

PROJECTING YOUR VOICE	Speaking with a loud, clear voice so the audience can hear and understand what is being said.
PROPERTIES	Things that can be moved easily around the stage and look as though they may belong to someone, also called PROPS.
PUBLICATION	A book, story, music, play or the like which is available to the public.
PUBLICITY	Letting people know you are doing something and would like them to come see it.
PUBLISHED	Printed material available to the public.
PUPPET SHOW	Performance where puppets tell the story.
PUPPETEER	Person who works the puppets, often providing the voice, too.
PYROTECHNICS	A fireworks show.
QUIRK	Odd habit, peculiar behavior, idiosyncrasy.
RAISED FLOOR	Section of floor that is higher than another area.
RAKE	Angle, slant.
RAKED STAGE	Stage that slants from the back of the stage down toward to front of the stage.
RANGE	Variety of acting ability.
READ FOR A PART	Reading the lines of a certain character at an audition.
READING	When actors sit or stand to say their lines, but are not blocked: also, short for STAGED READING.
REAL	Something that is true or the truth.
REALISTIC	Like the real thing.
RECOGNIZE	To know, to identify from past experience.
RECORD	To tape sound or music so it can be played back later; also to write down.
RECTANGLE	Figure with four sides with opposite sides being the same length.
REFERENCE	Source of information.
REFLECTED	Returning an image such as would be seen in a mirror.
REFRESHMENTS	Snacks and drinks often served during intermission.
REHEARSAL	To do over and over and over again until you have it the way you want it to be, see PRACTICE.

REHEARSAL SCHEDULE	Days and times practice is planned.
RELATIONSHIP	How one person is associated with another, such as brother and sister or student and teacher.
REMEMBER	Something you will need to know later and are careful not to forget.
REPERTOIRE	A collection of plays, scenes, songs or any other performance materials that are prepared and ready to perform at any time.
REQUIRE	Need, must try or should have.
RESEMBLE	Looks like or is similar to.
RESOLVES	Finishes, ends; to find a solution to.
RING	Circular area in which circuses traditionally perform.
RINGMASTER	Emcee/announcer of circus acts.
ROCK 'N' ROLL	Popular style of music that started in the 1950s.
ROLE	Character in a play, also called a PART.
ROLE PLAYING	Often the opportunity to act like another person and see things from their particular viewpoint; also sometimes called PLAY ACTING.
ROMAN NUMERALS	Letters from the ancient Roman alphabet that represent numbers: I, II, III, IV, V, etc.
RUN LINES	To practice reading a part with another person, a good way to memorize.
RUNNING CREW	Group that works in the backstage area during a show, also called the DECK CREW.
SAFETY	Making certain that no one will be harmed or hurt.
SATIRE	To make fun of certain people, thoughts, or ideas by pointing out how ridiculous they really are through writing, music and art.
SC.1	Short for SCENE ONE, often used on a rehearsal schedule to indicate what is being practiced.
SC.2	Short for SCENE TWO, often used on a rehearsal schedule to indicate what is being practiced.
SC.3	Short for SCENE THREE, often used on a rehearsal schedule to indicate what is being practiced.
SCENE	Grouping of lines that relate to a certain time or situation and tells part of a story.
SCENE ONE	First scene in an act.

SCENE TWO	Second scene in an act.
SCENE THREE	Third scene in an act.
SCENERY	Part of the set that shows the location of the scene or play, usually on the backdrop.
SCRIM	A thin cloth used for shadow puppet performances.
SCRIPT	Copy of the play from which the actors learn their lines.
SEASON	Winter, spring, summer or fall; also, a series of performances that are arranged to be done during a certain time period.
SEASONAL TIME	Times of the year: spring, summer, winter and fall.
SECONDARY	Coming after whatever is thought to be of first importance.
SECURE	Safe, stable, also, held together in place.
SERIOUS	Sincere, concerned, not funny.
SET	Various pieces on the stage that create the location of the show; also, to decide positions while blocking; also, to use powder to keep makeup on.
SET DESIGNER	Person who draws and makes the set for a show.
SET CHANGE	When the stage crew moves pieces of or the whole set between scenes or acts.
SETTING	Place where the story happens.
SEVERAL	More than two.
SHADOW PUPPETS	Forms that are used behind a screen, shade or thin curtain and have light projected on them from behind.
SHARE	To let someone help, use, offer their ideas or suggestions.
SHEET	Piece of cloth or fabric used on a bed to cover the mattress.
SHOW	Something people come to see in order to be entertained and/or informed; also, to DISPLAY.
SIGNIFICANT	Important to the situation or event.
SING	To use your voice to make music.
SKETCH	To quickly draw out an idea or design; also, scene that has a beginning, middle and an ending which is usually very silly, better known as a SKIT.
SKIT	Scene that has a beginning, middle and an ending which is usually very silly, also known as a SKETCH.
SLAP-STICK COMEDY	Style of comedy that is very big and silly, a farce.
SOFT SHOE	A quiet, subtle dance similar to tap.

SOLILOQUY	Long speech by one person who is talking to himself, sometimes also called a MONOLOG.
SOLO ACT	Performance featuring only one person, sometimes called ONE PERSON SHOW.
SONG	Musical number.
SOUND	Anything you hear.
SOUND CREW	Group that assists with the sound equipment for a show.
SOUND DESIGNER	Person who decides about all the sound needs for a show, also called AUDIO DESIGNER.
SOUND EQUIPMENT	Machines, electronics, cables and cords, anything that helps to produce sound for a show, same as AUDIO EQUIPMENT.
SOUND SYSTEM	How all the audio/sound equipment is organized to produce sound for the show, same as AUDIO SYSTEM.
SOUND TRACK	Music or special effects that are recorded and played back during a show.
SOUND WAVES	How sound travels through the air, similar to a surfboard on the ocean.
SPEAKER	Piece of sound equipment that allows the audience to hear the sound from the stage; also, someone who is talking to a group.
SPECIAL EFFECTS	Things that are done to create a surprise or make something look especially interesting or unusual.
SPECIALTY	An act that requires special skills or training to perform, often featured in a show.
SPONGE	Soft pad made especially for applying cream and greasepaint makeup.
SPONTANEOUS	Following your natural instincts in response to a situation without necessarily thinking them through.
SPOTLIGHT	Large light that is usually focused on an actor during a special moment.
STAGE	Any area where someone can perform, but traditionally thought of as having a raised floor and curtain.
STAGE BUSINESS	Little things that can make a character appear more realistic during a scene.
STAGE CREW	Name for all of the people who work backstage.
STAGE DIRECTION	To stand or move to a certain position on stage as instructed, also called BLOCKING or STAGING.
STAGE FLOOR	Ground area of the stage.

STAGE FRIGHT	Nervous jitters before going on stage, also known as BUTTERFLIES IN YOUR STOMACH.
STAGE LEFT	Left side of the stage as an actor looks at the audience.
STAGE MANAGER	Person who is in charge of the show when it is in performance and calls all cues.
STAGE RIGHT	Right side of the stage as an actor looks at the audience.
STAGE WHISPER	Very hushed spoken line, but loud enough for the audience to here and understand.
STAGED READING	Similar to a READING, except the actors are blocked and move about the stage while reading from scripts.
STAGING	To stand or move to a certain position on stage as instructed, also called BLOCKING or STAGE DIRECTION.
STAR	Person about whom the story of the show is about, also called a LEADING PLAYER or PRINCIPAL. Called a STAR because they shine so brightly in their performance.
STATIC	Non-moving.
STEP INTO	Taking over a part or position.
STICK PUPPETS	Dolls that are on sticks, usually with loose arms and legs that bounce when stick is moved up and down.
STORY	Telling of events and happenings, can be true or untrue.
STORYLINE	How a story goes from beginning to middle to end, same as PLOT.
STREET PERFORMERS	Entertainers who can create a stage anywhere and perform a show.
STRETCH	To make tighter, wider or longer by pulling.
STRING SECTION	Part of an orchestra made up of violins, violas, cellos and stringed basses.
STROBE LIGHTS	Special light that can flash on and off at different rates and creates the effect of slow motion.
STYLE	Special way of doing something.
SUBPLOT	Secondary storyline.
SUCCESSION	Following.
SUPERSTITION	Ideas about the way certain things should or shouldn't be done in order to avoid bad luck.
SUPPLIES	Items needed to be collected to work on a project.
SUPPORT BOARDS	Pieces of wood that help to hold something up.
SUPPORT SYSTEM	Pieces that are used to help stand something up.

SUPPORTING LEAD	Person who is important to the story, but not the center of it, same as SUPPORTING PLAYER.
SUPPORTING PLAYER	Person who is important to the story, but not the center of it, same as SUPPORTING LEAD.
SWING	Person who learns all the chorus roles and goes on in the show when needed.
SWING DANCE	Dance style popular during the 1940s — World War II era.
SYNOPSIS	Quick telling of a story and all the highlights.
SYSTEM	Grouping of related items that work together for a specific function.
TALL	How high something is.
TAP DANCE	Dance style that uses special shoes to create sounds when the feet are touched to the floor.
TAPE RECORDER	Piece of equipment that can save sounds and play them back at a later time.
TEAM	Group that works together for a common purpose.
TEAM EFFORT	When everybody works together for a common goal.
TECHNICAL	Having to do with equipment.
TECHNIQUE	Particular skills.
TERM	Special word used to describe something particular.
THE END	Where a story finishes.
THE FOURTH WALL	Invisible wall that separates the audience from the actors on stage.
THE HOUSE	Where the audience sits.
THEATRE	Building where shows are performed; also, in general, anything having to do with performance.
THEATRICAL	Often refers to manner in which a presentation is made, particularly if it incorporates many elements associated with theatre such as lighting, costuming and makeup.
THRUST STAGE	Stage where the audience can sit around three sides.
TIDY	To clean up.
TIGHTROPE WALKER	Performer who works on a tightrope, usually in the circus, also called HIGH-WIRE ARTIST.
TIME	Happening on a certain day and/or part of the day; also, hour, minute or second.

TINT	To give a slight color.
TITLE	Name of the story.
TO ENTER	When an actor comes out onto the stage.
TO EXIT	When an actor leaves the stage.
TO STORE	To put things away.
TOUCH-UP	To fix so nothing is missed, overlooked or left unfinished.
TRADITION	An established ceremony, ritual, activity or story from a previous generation.
TRADITIONAL	Something that has happened the same way over and over again, probably for many years.
TRANSACTION	Action between two or more parties.
TRANSPARENT	Able to see through.
TRAPEZE ARTIST	Performer who works on a trapeze above the ground, usually in the circus.
TRAVELER CURTAINS	Smaller theatrical curtains, often hung in fly gallery, and able to move as needed.
TREE	Special stand that holds light and is usually set up in the wings to light the stage.
TRIANGLE	Three-sided shape.
TUBE	Long, round container.
TWO ACT PLAY	Show that appears in two halves, usually with an intermission between.
UNCONSCIOUS	Not aware.
UNDERSTUDY	Person who learns all the lead, supporting and featured roles and goes on stage when needed.
UPSTAGE	Point furthest away from the audience on stage.
USUALLY	Way something is almost all of the time.
UTILITARIAN	Useful in many capacities.
VALIDATE	To give credit for or approve of.
VIDEO	Tape that can be recorded onto and watched later.
VIGNETTE	Short scene.
VISUAL	Something that can be seen.

VOCABULARY	Collection of words.
VOLUME	Softness or loudness of sound.
WARDROBE	Collection of costumes.
WARDROBE CREW	Group who handles all the costumes and repairs to them.
WASH-OUT	When someone's face cannot be seen from the audience because the lighting is too bright or their makeup is not dark enough.
WATER-BASED	Makeup that already has water in it or can be used with water to apply.
WHITEFACE	Special makeup that will make entire face very white, most often used by clowns and mimes.
WIDE	Measurement of something from side to side.
WIDTH	How wide something is.
WIG	Fake hair.
WIG CAP	Small piece of nylon that hair can be tucked into for use under a wig.
WIG DESIGNER	Person who is in charge of creating all the wigs in a show.
WIG PINS	Special pins that will not damage wigs when used.
WINGS	Sides of the stage, usually hidden by the legs.
WOODEN FRAME	Structure over which cloth is stretched to make a flat.
WORK	Undertaking a task requiring either physical or mental application.

Index

About the Author

Adrea Gibbs is a fifth-generation Californian whose first theatrical experience was appearing in the "Rocking Horse Dance" as part of an Arcadia (California) Parks and Recreation Dance recital at the tender age of five.

She has had the good fortune to travel and live across the United States, Europe and Asia in a variety of capacities tied to entertainment, from performance to management.

She has appeared in three companies of *CATS* and The German National Company's production of *Starlight Express*. She was a trapeze artist with Troupe Hertz in the Moscow Circus, "Polly" in *Crazy for You*, and Princess Leia for the grand opening of *Star Tours* at Disneyland.

As a director and choreographer, she has created performances for the German and Czech Cultural Ministries, the Musical Theatre Guild (MTG), Walt Disney World, Disneyland, EuroDisneyland, the Cabrillo Music Theatre, Window On China and many other independent plays, musicals and special events.

Ms. Gibbs' love of working with children has prompted her to teach and develop programs for the Gymboree Corporation. She has also worked as Program Director for the Boys & Girls Club of Hollywood, instructed Moorpark Melodrama children's workshops, and taught everything from pre-school to college level classes and workshops ranging from dance and theatre to makeup and music performance.

She is currently the Director of Children's Programming for Oakridge Athletic Club in Simi Valley, California. Ms. Gibbs will soon have a Ph.D. in communications from Columbus University.

Order Form

Meriwether Publishing Ltd.
PO Box 7710
Colorado Springs CO 80933-7710
Phone: 800-937-5297 Fax: 719-594-9916
Website: www.meriwether.com

Please send me the following books:

_____ **Let's Put on a Show! #BK-B231**   **$19.95**
by Adrea Gibbs
A beginner's theatre handbook for young actors

_____ **Introduction to Theatre Arts —**   **$19.95**
Student Handbook #BK-B264
by Suzi Zimmerman
A 36-week action handbook for theatre arts instruction

_____ **Introduction to Theatre Arts —**   **$24.95**
Teacher's Guide #BK-B265
by Suzi Zimmerman
Teacher's guide to Introduction to Theatre Arts

_____ **The Theatre and You #BK-B115**   **$17.95**
by Marsh Cassady
An introductory text on all aspects of theatre

_____ **Everything About Theatre #BK-B200**   **$19.95**
by Robert L. Lee
The guidebook of theatre fundamentals

_____ **Theatre Games for Young Performers**   **$16.95**
#BK-B188
by Maria C. Novelly
Improvisations and exercises for developing acting skills

_____ **Acting Games — Improvisations and**   **$16.95**
Exercises #BK-B168
by Marsh Cassady
A textbook of theatre games and improvisations

These and other fine Meriwether Publishing books are available at your local bookstore or direct from the publisher. Prices subject to change without notice. Check our website or call for current prices.

Name: _____ e-mail: _____

Organization name: _____

Address: _____

City: _____ State: _____

Zip: _____ Phone: _____

   ❑ **Check enclosed**

   ❑ **Visa / MasterCard / Discover #** _____

                                   Expiration
Signature: _____ *date:* _____

        (required for credit card orders)

Colorado residents: Please add 3% sales tax.
Shipping: Include $3.95 for the first book and 75¢ for each additional book ordered.

   ❑ *Please send me a copy of your complete catalog of books and plays.*

Order Form

Meriwether Publishing Ltd.
PO Box 7710
Colorado Springs CO 80933-7710
Phone: 800-937-5297 Fax: 719-594-9916
Website: www.meriwether.com

Please send me the following books:

_____ **Let's Put on a Show! #BK-B231** $19.95
by Adrea Gibbs
A beginner's theatre handbook for young actors

_____ **Introduction to Theatre Arts —** $19.95
Student Handbook #BK-B264
by Suzi Zimmerman
A 36-week action handbook for theatre arts instruction

_____ **Introduction to Theatre Arts —** $24.95
Teacher's Guide #BK-B265
by Suzi Zimmerman
Teacher's guide to Introduction to Theatre Arts

_____ **The Theatre and You #BK-B115** $17.95
by Marsh Cassady
An introductory text on all aspects of theatre

_____ **Everything About Theatre #BK-B200** $19.95
by Robert L. Lee
The guidebook of theatre fundamentals

_____ **Theatre Games for Young Performers** $16.95
#BK-B188
by Maria C. Novelly
Improvisations and exercises for developing acting skills

_____ **Acting Games — Improvisations and** $16.95
Exercises #BK-B168
by Marsh Cassady
A textbook of theatre games and improvisations

These and other fine Meriwether Publishing books are available at your local bookstore or direct from the publisher. Prices subject to change without notice. Check our website or call for current prices.

Name: _____ e-mail: _____

Organization name: _____

Address: _____

City: _____ State: _____

Zip: _____ Phone: _____

❑ **Check enclosed**
❑ **Visa / MasterCard / Discover #** _____

Expiration
date:
Signature: _____ _____
(required for credit card orders)

Colorado residents: Please add 3% sales tax.
Shipping: Include $3.95 for the first book and 75¢ for each additional book ordered.

❑ *Please send me a copy of your complete catalog of books and plays.*